JOIN IN

Developing Conversation Strategies

1 Student Book

Jack C. Richards
& Kerry O'Sullivan

OXFORD
UNIVERSITY PRESS

OXFORD
UNIVERSITY PRESS

198 Madison Avenue
New York, NY 10016 USA

Great Clarendon Street, Oxford OX2 6DP UK

Oxford University Press is a department of the University of Oxford.
It furthers the University's objective of excellence in research, scholarship,
and education by publishing worldwide in

Oxford   New York

Auckland   Cape Town   Dar es Salaam   Hong Kong   Karachi
Kuala Lumpur   Madrid   Melbourne   Mexico City   Nairobi
New Delhi   Shanghai   Taipei   Toronto

With offices in

Argentina   Austria   Brazil   Chile   Czech Republic   France   Greece
Guatemala   Hungary   Italy   Japan   Poland   Portugal   Singapore
South Korea   Switzerland   Thailand   Turkey   Ukraine   Vietnam

OXFORD and OXFORD ENGLISH are registered trademarks of
Oxford University Press

© Oxford University Press 2009

Database right Oxford University Press (maker)

No unauthorized photocopying

Editorial Director: Laura Pearson
Executive Publishing Manager: Laura Le Dréan
Senior Managing Editor: Pat O'Neill
Director, ADP: Susan Sanguily
Design Manager: Stacy Merlin
Designer: Sangeeta E. Ramcharan
Cover design: Michael Steinhofer
Image Editor: Robin Fadool
Project Leader, ADP: Bridget McGoldrick
Manufacturing Manager: Shanta Persaud
Senior Manufacturing Controller: Eve Wong

ISBN (STUDENT BOOK): 978 0 19 436775 2
ISBN (STUDENT BOOK WITH CD): 978 0 19 446050 7

Printed in China.

10 9 8 7 6 5 4 3 2

ACKNOWLEDGMENTS

Illustrations by: Adrian Barclay: 9; Barbara Bastian: 62; 68; 82; Kenneth Batelman:
26; 37; 42; 44 (bottom); 80; Grace Chen: 4; 5; 23; 59; 65; 77 (bottom);
Marcos Chin: 8; 53; 60; KS Chung: 25; 48; 55; Mona Daly/Mendola Art, 14; 77;
Kevin Hopgood: 20; 69; Kim Johnson/Lindgren & Smith, 16; 45; 53 (bottom); 65
(top); Karen Minot: 20 (bottom); 56 (bottom); 74; Marc Mones/American Artist
Reps: 19 (bottom); 30; 66; Christian Musselman: 31; 51; 63; Leif Peng: 57;
Jorge Santillan/Beehive Illustration: 6; 47; 52; 75; Phil Scheuer: 17 (bottom); 38;
79; Rob Schuster: 19; 47 (bottom); 49; Kaylene Simmons/Lemonade Illustration
Agency: 17; 18; William Waitzman: 44; Laurence Whitely/NB Illustration: 50; 71.

We would like to thank the following for their permission to reproduce photographs:

Cover: First row from left to right: Blend Images/Jupiter Images; Photo Alto/
Jupiter Images; Second row: Grapheast/Alamy: Jan Kassay; BrandX/Jupiter
Images; Bottom row: Dex Image/Jupiter Images; Taxi/DreamPictures/Getty
Images; Hemera/Age FotoStock: (person holding CD); istockphoto.com: (CD).

Interior: A1PIX Ltd. Digital Picture Library/Superbild: 15 (café); Age FotoStock:
P. Narayan: 13; Age FotoStock: Jeff Greenberg, 15 (ice cream shop and
department store); Corbis/Age FotoStock: Steve Prezant, 21 (barbeque);
ThinkStock/Age FotoStock: 33 (security guard); BlueMoon Stock/ Age FotoStock:
Chad Coleman, 54 (water skiing); Age FotoStock: Roy Ooms, 56 (ice hockey);
Alamy: David R. Frazier Photolibrary, Inc./Alamy; 12; Alamy: Dennis Cox, 13;
Alamy: Howard Barlow, 15 (Internet café); Alamy: Richard Levine, 15 (electronics
store); Alamy: Chris Cheadle, 15 (clothing store); Alamy: Frances Roberts , 21
(fashion show); MasPix/Alamy: 21 (soccer game); foodfolio / Alamy: 27 (soda);
Blickwinkel/Alamy: 33 (hotel clerk); Alamy: Daniel Hurst 39 (park); Visions
of America, LLC/Alamy: 39 (stadium); avatra images/Alamy: 54 (jogging); Aflo
Foto Agency/Alamy: 56 (tennis); dbimages/Alamy: 67 (Vienamese handicrafts);
amana images inc./Alamy: 73; Jupiter Images/Creatas/Alamy: 76; Associated
Press: Markus Stuecklin, 21 (IT Fair); Danita Delimont: Jon Arnold Images/Danita
Delimont: 12; Danita Delimont: John Warburton-Lee, 56 (white-water rafting);
Getty Images: Stone/Getty Images: Robin Smith, 21 (roller coaster); Sebun Photo/
Getty Images: 39 (bridge); Getty Images: Tyler Stableford, 54 (rock climbing);
ImageState: ImageState: Ethel Davies, 14 Mexico City; Photonica/Getty Images:
Philip J Brittan, 36 (ATM); InMagine: Corbis/InMagine: 36 (Internet café and
taxi stand); inMagine: 50 (student); DigitalVision/InMagine: 56 (ice skating);
Thinkstock/InMagine: 56 (skiing); istockphoto.com: 7; 11; 61; 67; Jupiter Images
FAN Travelstock/Jupiter Images: Andrew Walsh, 21 (dance club); Corbis/Jupiter
Images: 33 (Vet); Tetra Images/Jupiter Images: Erik Isakson, 33 (DJ); BlendImages/
Jupiter Images: 35 (music teacher); Blend Images/Jupiter Images: Andersen Ross,
35 (DJ); LWA/Blend Images/Jupiter Images: 54 (ice skating); Blend Images/Jupiter
Images: 72 (college student); Masterfile: 15 (bookstore); 28; 33 (tour guide);
Masterfile: George Simhoni, 39 (train station); Masterfile: Jeremy Woodhouse, 39
(museum); Masterfile: Greg Scott, 67 (canal tour); Photo Edit Inc./Spencer Grant,
15 (music store); Photo Edit Inc.: Susan van Etten, 15 (sporting goods store); Photo
Edit Inc.: Cindy Charles, 33 (rock musician); Photo Edit Inc.: Michael Newman,
33 (travel agent); Photo Edit Inc.: Rudi Von Briel, 37 (subway station); Photo
Edit Inc.: David R. Frazier, 54 (swimming); Photo Edit Inc.: Mary Kate Denny,
72 (adult education students); Photo Edit Inc.: David Young-Wolff, 72 (grade
school students); PunchStock: 24 (cookie); PhotoDisc/PunchStock: 24 (mixed
nuts); PunchStock: 33 (flight attendant); Corbis/PunchStock: 39 (apt. building);
Robert Fried Photography: 36 (food stall); RobertStock: Daniel Hurst, 24 (soda);
Daniel Hurst, 24 (fruit); Shutterstock: 24 (tea); 24 (milk); 27; (grilled chicken with
vegetables); 39 (temple); StockFood: Lew Robertson, 27 (fish with rice); Food
Image Source/Foodfolio Studios/Stockfood: 27 (steak with French fries);
Jim Scherer Photography/Stockfood: 27 (banana split); Stockfood: Lew Robertson,
27 (tomato soup); Louis Wallach Photography/Stockfood: 27 (slice of apple pie);
Eising Food Photography/Stockfood: 27 (salad); Superstock: Age Fotostock /
SuperStock: 64; Pacific Stock/SuperStock: 67 (Ho Chi Minh Memorial); The Image
Works: The Image Works: Joe Sohm, 12; The Image Works: Thomas Pflaum, 21
(movie theater); The Image Works: David R. Frazier, 21 (science museum); The
Image Works: Norbert von der Groeben, 33 (computer programmer); The Image
Works:David R. Frazier, 35 (flight attendant); The Image Works: Jeff Greenberg,
35 (singer); The Image Works: Bob Daemmrich, 41; The Image Works: Rob
Crandall, 43 (tall apt. building); The Image Works: James Marshall, 43 (small
apt. building); The Image Works: Bob Daemmrich, 46; The Image Works: Jeff
Greenberg, 54 (canoeing); The Image Works: Jeff Greenberg, 56 (canoeing); The
Image Works: Bob Daemmrich, 72 (junior high school students and high school
students); Veer: 10; 36; Photodisc/Veer: 39 (statue and fountain).

*The publisher would like to thank the following for their help in developing this
series:* Matt Caldwell, Hannan University, Japan; Cheng-Chi Chan, School of
Continuing Education, Chinese Cultural University, Taiwan; William Davis,
Daejin University, Korea; Duane Dunston, UBest Language School/Chang-Shing
Senior High School; Taiwan; Janet M.D. Higgins, Okinawa University, Japan;
Tom Harper, Taiwan; Ward Ketcheson, Aomori University, Japan; Daniel T. Kirk,
Yokkaichi University, Japan; Kevin Lee, Kyung Hee University, Korea; Crystal Lin,
Tzu Chi University, Taiwan; Rick Romanko, Wayo Women's University, Japan;
David Ruzicka, Shinshu University, Japan; Stephen Shucart, Akita Prefectural
University, Japan; Helen Song, Sisa Language Institute, Korea; Keum Ok Song,
BCM Language School, Korea; Ha Jung Sung, Chungnam National University,
Korea; Damien Tresize, Leader College of Management, Tainan, Taiwan; Hajime
Uematsu, Hirosaki University, Japan; Tamami Wada, Nagoya Gakuin University,
Japan; Ching-ping Wang, Tunghai University, Taiwan; J. Scott Wigenton,
Woosong University, Korea; Catherine Yang, North Taiwan Institute
of Technology; Rick Yang, Gram English School; Jeffrey Lehman, LRD School;
Soo Ha Yim, Hanyang University International Language Institute, Korea.

Introduction

Welcome to *Join In*. This is a three-level speaking and listening series that teaches an important aspect of English: developing conversation strategies for *what* to say and also *how* to say it. This will help you improve your English.

Student Book

There are two lessons in each of the 12 units in the Student Book. Each lesson focuses on a different aspect of the unit topic. The lessons are organized into five sections, each one with carefully graded activities that provide opportunities to speak and listen.

Lesson 1

Lesson 1 begins with a conversation. It presents language and grammar that will be practiced throughout the lesson in context. **Language Focus** presents and provides practice with a grammar point. The **Listen and Understand** activities provide practice with a variety of listening skills. These activities will help you improve your overall listening comprehension skills.

Lesson 2

Lesson 2 introduces more vocabulary related to the unit topic. **Conversation Strategy** focuses on a feature of spoken English and provides examples of how to say what you want to say. Using these strategies will help you speak English in a more natural way. The **Listen and Understand** activities provide practice with a variety of listening skills. These activities will help you improve your overall listening comprehension skills.

Join In

Join In, the last section in each lesson, gives you the chance to speak to your classmates about the lesson topic. It also lets you practice the language focus and conversation strategy from earlier in the lesson.

Audio Program

There are various types of spoken English on the CDs including casual conversations, telephone conversations, interviews, and messages. The complete audio program for the Student Book is on the Class CDs. There is also a Student CD on the inside back cover of this Student Book for self study. The Student CD contains the Conversations from page 1 of each unit (the conversation from part B and the practices from Part C).

Scope and Sequence

Unit	Lesson	Language Focus	Conversation Strategy
1 Meeting people page 6	1 Nice to meet you.	Yes/No questions	
	2 Making small talk		showing interest
2 Interesting Places page 12	1 Where are you from?	*be* + adjective	
	2 Favorite places in a city		asking follow-up questions
3 Routines and Times page 18	1 Daily routines	adverbs of frequency	
	2 Going out with friends		accepting and declining invitations
4 Foods and Meals page 24	1 Likes and dislikes	count and non-count nouns	
	2 Eating out		confirming information
5 Occupations page 30	1 Finding out what people do	*Wh-* questions	
	2 Giving opinions		agreeing and disagreeing
6 Going Places page 36	1 Where's the subway station?	*there is/there are* + prepositions of place	
	2 Finding places		checking information
7 Home Life page 42	1 Homes and apartments	questions with *is there* and *does*	
	2 Homestay		asking for permission
8 Possessions page 48	1 Keeping in touch	adverb phrases	
	2 Cool things		expressing enthusiasm
9 Enjoying the outdoors page 54	1 Seasonal activities	verb + gerund	
	2 Weekend activities		using echo questions
10 Shopping page 60	1 Prices	questions with *how much*	
	2 Buying things in a store		reacting to opinions
11 Tourism page 66	1 Things to see	modal verbs	
	2 On vacation		giving more information
12 Biographies page 72	1 Childhood days	past tense	
	2 Events to remember		responding and asking for more information

1 CLASSROOM LANGUAGE

A. Use the expressions below to complete the conversations.

What's this called in English?   *What does cheap mean?*   *Could you repeat that?*

What's a vet?   *How do you pronounce this word?*   *How do you spell that?*

1. **A:** _____
    B: Which word? This one?
    A: Uh-huh. That one.
    B: Pilates.

2. **A:** _____
    B: It means *not expensive.*

3. **A:** _____
    B: A doctor for animals. It's short for *veterinarian.*
    A: _____
    B: V-e-t-e-r-i-n-a-r-i-a-n.

4. **A:** _____
    B: This? It's called a tennis racket.
    A: I'm sorry. _____
    B: Tennis racket.

CD 1 Track 2 **B.** Listen and check your answers.

C. Pairs. Practice the dialogues above. Take turns.

2 SPELLING

 Track 3 **A.** Listen and practice saying the alphabet.

Aa	Bb	Cc	Dd	Ee	Ff	Gg
Hh	Ii	Jj	Kk	Ll	Mm	Nn
Oo	Pp	Qq	Rr	Ss	Tt	Uu
Vv	Ww	Xx	Yy	Zz		

 Track 4 **B.** Listen and complete the missing information.

First name: P-A-_____-T-_____

Last name: _____-R-_____-Y

C. Pairs. Ask your partner how to spell his or her name. Take turns.

Track 5 **A.** Listen and practice saying the numbers.

 Track 6 **B.** Listen and practice saying the days of the week.

Monday   Tuesday   Wednesday   Thursday   Friday   Saturday   Sunday

C. Pairs. Ask and answer these questions.

1. What days do you have English class?
2. What days do you study?
3. What days are the weekend?
4. What days are weekdays?

Track 7 **D.** Listen and complete these phone numbers.

Name	Phone number
1. Mary	__65-3__-633
2. Jack	2__-726-63__
3. Jun	8__3-77__-4__9

Track 8 **A.** Listen and practice saying the times.

It's four o'clock.

It's seven ten.

It's eight fifteen.

It's six thirty.

It's one fifty.

It's nine forty-five.

B. Pairs. Look at these times. Say what time it is.

1. **A:** What time is it?
   B: It's _____

3. **A:** What time is it?
   B: It's _____

2. **A:** What time is it?
   B: It's _____

4. **A:** What time is it?
   B: It's _____

C. Pairs. Ask and answer these questions.

1. What time does English class start?
2. What time does class end?

unit

1 Meeting People

LESSON 1: Nice to meet you

1 INTRODUCTIONS

A. Look at people meeting each other for the first time. In your country, how do you greet people when you meet them for the first time? Check (✓) the greeting you use most often.

 Track 9 **B.** Pairs. Listen to the conversation. Then practice with a partner.

A: Excuse me. 1 Are you Ted?

B: No, I'm Bill. 2 That's Ted over there.

A: Oh, yeah. Anyway, my name's Suzie.

B: Hi, Suzie. 3 How are you? Are you in my Spanish class?

A: Yes, I am.

B: *Hola!*

C. Pairs. Practice the conversation again. Use this information.

Practice 1

1 Is your name Brian?

2 Brian's the guy over there.

3 Nice to meet you.

Practice 2

1 Is your name Ricardo?

2 Ric's not here yet.

3 How are things?

D. Class activity. Use the example language below to meet your classmates.

A: Hi. Are you _____?

B: No, I'm not. I'm _____.

A: Nice to meet you. My name's _____.

Track 10 **A. Listen and practice.**

Are you Jack?	Yes, I am.
	No, I'm not.
Is your last name Wong?	Yes, it is.
	No, it isn't.
Is he Peter?	Yes, he is.
Is she Marie?	No, she's not.
Are you a student?	Yes, I am.
	No, I'm not.

 Track 11 **B. Pairs. Complete the conversations with words from A. Listen and check your answers. Then practice with a partner.**

1. **A:** Is your first name Amy?
   B: No, it _____. It's Emily.

2. **A:** Are you Bill?
   B: No, _____ not. I'm Ted.

3. **A:** Is the teacher's first name Peter?
   B: No, it _____. It's Patrick.

4. **A:** Are you a tennis player?
   B: No, _____ not. I play basketball.

5. **A:** Is the teacher from Canada?
   B: No, she's _____. She's from Australia.

6. **A:** Is your last name Jackson?
   B: No, it isn't. _____ Johnson.

C. Pairs. Take turns asking and answering the questions above, using true information.

CD 1 Track 12 **A.** Listen and complete the missing information.

1.

first name:

_____

last/family name:

_____

home phone number:

_____

2.

first name:

_____

last/family name:

_____

home phone number:

_____

B. Listen again. Where do the conversations take place?

1. **a.** at a library   **b.** at a bank   **c.** at a computer center

2. **a.** at a library   **b.** at a bank   **c.** at a computer center

4 JOIN IN

A. Answer these questions. Write your answers in the spaces provided.

First name: _____   Last name: _____

Are you...

a teacher? _____

a tennis player?_____

from Canada? _____

a college student? _____

a basketball player?_____

(your idea)? _____

B. Pairs. Talk to a classmate. Introduce yourself, then ask and answer the questions from A.

A: Hi, I'm Fu-an.

B: Hi, Fu-an. I'm Ken. Nice to meet you.

A: Nice to meet you too. Are you a student?

1 LEISURE ACTIVITIES

  Track 13 **A.** Circle the types of activities you like. Then listen and repeat.

1. television	**4.** baseball	**7.** reading	**10.** classical
2. shopping	**5.** tennis	**8.** eating out	**11.** jazz
3. swimming	**6.** video games	**9.** country	**12.** rock

B. Write the words from **A** in the correct category. Then check (✓) the things you do.

Sports	Music	Other activities

C. Pairs. What leisure activities do you like? Talk with a partner.

A: Do you like music?

B: Yes, I like classical. Do you?

A: No, I don't. I like _____ .

2 CONVERSATION STRATEGY: SHOWING INTEREST

 Track 14

A. Pairs. Listen to the conversations. Then practice with a partner.

1. **A:** Do you play a musical instrument?
   B: Yes, I do. I play the trumpet.
   A: *Really?*

2. **A:** Do you like rock music?
   B: Yeah, I love it. My mom is a rock singer.
   A: *Cool.*

B. Notice how we use expressions such as *really* and *cool* to show interest in what people say. We can also use these expressions:

That's nice.   *That's interesting.*   *Is that right?*   *Wow!*

Pairs. Now practice the conversations in A again, using different expressions to show interest.

C. Pairs. Use words from B to show interest in these conversations. Then practice with a partner and add information of your own.

1. **A:** Do you play volleyball?
   B: Yes, I'm on the school team.
   A: _____.

2. **A:** Do you like sports?
   B: Yes, I play tennis every day.
   A: _____.

3. **A:** Do you play video games?
   B: Yes, I have 10 Nintendo Wii games.
   A: _____.

D. Pairs. Practice the conversations from A again. This time use your own information.

3 LISTEN AND UNDERSTAND

 Track 15 **A. Listen to people talking about the things they like. Number three of the words from 1 to 3 in the order you hear them.**

1. ___ country   ___ rock   ___ hip-hop   ___ classical   ___ jazz
2. ___ football   ___ basketball   ___ tennis   ___ volleyball   ___ baseball
3. ___ video games   ___ TV   ___ cooking   ___ eating out   ___ shopping

B. Listen again. Number three of the expressions of interest from 1 to 3 in the order you hear them.

____ Oh, that's nice.   ____ That's interesting.
____ Is that right?   ____ Cool!

4 JOIN IN

A. Groups. Which sports are popular at your school? Work together to make a list of the popular sports.

B. Class activity. Talk with your classmates and agree on a list of sports that are popular at your school. Put them in order from most popular to least popular.

unit 2 Interesting Places

LESSON 1: Where are you from?

1 MY HOMETOWN

A. What do you think? Number the pictures below. (Pictures can have more than one number.)

1. interesting   **3.** clean   **5.** exciting

2. beautiful   **4.** crowded   **6.** big

Toronto

Bangkok

Chicago

 Track 16 **B. Pairs. Listen to the conversation. Then practice with a partner.**

A: 1 Where are you from, Ted?

B: I'm from Toronto.

A: Oh, Toronto. What's it like?

B: 2 Oh, It's a great city. I love it.

A: Yeah, I hear it's nice.

C. Pairs. Practice the conversation again. Use this information.

Practice 1

1 Where do you come from?

2 It's an interesting place.

Practice 2

1 Whereabouts are you from?

2 It's a wonderful place.

D. Groups. Choose three towns or cities in your country. What do your classmates think of them? Use these expressions.

It's not bad.

It's a great place.

It's boring.

2 LANGUAGE FOCUS: *BE* + ADJECTIVE

A. Listen and practice.

What's Toronto like?	It's an *interesting* city.
	It's very *interesting*.
What's your hometown like?	It's not an *interesting* city.
	It's not very *interesting*.

B. Pairs. Complete the conversations with items from A and the words below. Listen and check your answers. (Different answers are possible.) Then practice with a partner.

1. **A:** What's Hong Kong _____?
   B: It's a very _____ city.

2. **A:** _____ Los Angeles like?
   B: It's a great city. It's very _____.

3. **A:** What's Kyoto like?
   B: _____ a beautiful city. It's _____ very big.

4. **A:** What's Singapore like?
   B: It's a _____ city and it's very _____.

5. **A:** What's Shanghai _____?
   B: It's a _____ city and it's very crowded.

Try these

exciting	big
beautiful	clean
crowded	interesting

C. Pairs. Choose four places in your country or other places you and your partner know. Then take turns asking and answering questions.

A: *What's Beijing like?*
B: *It's a very interesting city. Parts of it are very old and parts of it are very new. But it's really crowded.*
A: *Really?*

Try these

| modern | quiet |
| expensive | noisy |

3 LISTEN AND UNDERSTAND

CD 1 Track 19 **A.** Listen to people talking about places. Number three of the words from 1 to 3 in the order you hear them.

1. ___ interesting   ___ crowded   ___ boring   ___ expensive   ___ favorite
2. ___ old   ___ crowded   ___ beautiful ___ expensive   ___ interesting
3. ___ wonderful   ___ exciting ___ expensive ___ crowded   ___ big

B. Listen again. Does the other person have the same opinion? Check (✓) your answers.

1. ☐ same   ☐ different   3. ☐ same   ☐ different
2. ☐ same   ☐ different

4 JOIN IN

A. Think of three interesting cities in different parts of the world. Write a few sentences about each place like this (but don't say the name of the place).

A: This is a very big city. It's crowded, but it's very beautiful. It's south of the U.S.

1. _____
2. _____
3. _____

B. Pairs. Take turns reading your descriptions from A to your partner. Can she or he guess the city you are thinking of?

B: Is it Los Angeles?
A: No, it isn't.
B: Is it Mexico City?
A: Yes, that's right.

1 STORES AND SHOPS

  Track 20 A. Circle the places you went to last week. Then listen and repeat.

1. Internet cafe

2. music store

3. bookstore

4. electronics store

5. cafe

6. sporting goods store

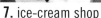

7. ice-cream shop

8. department store

9. clothing store

B. **Pairs. How often do you go to the places above? Check (✓) each place in A, then discuss your answers with your partner.**

Often ✓ ✓ ✓   Sometimes ✓ ✓   Not very often ✓

A: How often do you go to an Internet cafe?
B: Sometimes. I guess about once a week. How about you?
A: Oh, not very often. About once a month.

C. **Groups. Are there other types of stores and shops you like to go to? Tell your group where you like to shop. Use expressions of interest to keep the conversation going.**

A. **Pairs. Listen to the conversations. Then practice with a partner.**

1. **A:** What's your favorite Internet cafe?
   B: I guess my favorite is Bob's Internet Cafe. It's nice and quiet. *What's yours?*
   A: Mine is Downtown Internet Center. It's very cheap.

2. **A:** What's your favorite ice-cream shop?
   B: It's called Ice Cream Heaven. *How about you?*
   A: It's my favorite too! I love the chocolate delight.

B. **Notice how we use expressions such as *What's yours?* and *How about you?* to keep a conversation going. We can also use these expressions:**

What about you?   *And yours?*   *What's your favorite?*

Pairs. Now practice the conversations in A again, using different expressions to keep the conversation going.

C. **Pairs. Use words from B to keep these conversations going. Then practice with a partner and add information of your own.**

1. **A:** What's your favorite cafe?
   B: I like Norbucks Cafe. They have great coffee.
   _____?
   A: My favorite is College Cafe. All my friends hang out there.

2. **A:** My favorite clothing store is Friendly Fashions. They have really cool clothes. _____?
   B: I often shop at Sweet 17. The guys there are really cute.

D. **Pairs. Practice the conversations from A again. This time use your own information.**

3 LISTEN AND UNDERSTAND

A. What things do you think are important in a successful department store? Check (✓) the three things that are most important to you.

1. ____ prices are good
2. ____ the location is good
3. ____ the service is good
4. ____ a good selection of items
5. ____ it's a good size
6. ____ the staff are friendly

CD 1 Track 22

B. Listen to people talking about some of their favorite places. Number three of the places they talk about from 1 to 3 in the order you hear them.

____ bookstore   ____ ice-cream store

____ music store   ____ clothing store

C. Listen again. What do they like about each place?

1. a. ____ the price   b. ____ the size
2. a. ____ the choice   b. ____ the service
3. a. ____ the location   b. ____ the staff

4 JOIN IN

A. What's your opinion? Complete this survey.

My favorite place for coffee:_____

My favorite bookstore:_____

My favorite department store:_____

A good place for sporting goods:_____

My favorite music store:_____

A good place to buy computer games:_____

B. Pairs. Compare your answers from A with a partner.

A: My favorite place for coffee is Jo's. They have good iced coffee. What's yours?

B: Mine is King's. The snacks are delicious.

A: I think a good place for sporting goods is...

B: Really? I think...

unit 3 Routines and Times

LESSON 1: Daily routines

1 LET'S GET TOGETHER.

A. Number the pictures below. Then listen and repeat.

1. have coffee   2. have a snack   3. send a text message   4. make a phone call

 B. Pairs. Listen to the conversation. Then practice with a partner.

A: Hi. **1** How are things?

B: Pretty good, thanks.

A: Say, what are you doing later today?

B: Oh, nothing much.

A: Great. **2** Let's have a coffee after work.

B: Sure.

A: What time do you usually finish? Do you usually work late?

B: I usually finish around 6.

A: Great. **3** Text me when you finish, and we can get together.

C. Pairs. Practice the conversation again. Use this information.

Practice 1
1 How's everything?
2 Let's grab a bite to eat after work.
3 Give me a call when you finish.

Practice 2
1 How are you doing?
2 Let's go downtown later.
3 I'll call you later.

D. Class activity. What are you doing later today? Talk with your classmates and make plans to meet.

Track 24 **A.** **Listen and practice.**

Do you *usually* work late?	Yes, I do. No, I don't.		
What time do you *usually* finish work?	I	*always* *usually* *often* *sometimes* *never*	finish work around 6.

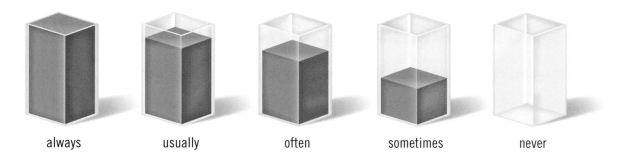

always   usually   often   sometimes   never

 Track 25 **B.** **Pairs. Complete the conversations with items from A and the words below. Listen and check your answers. Then practice with a partner.**

1. **A:** Do you usually get up early?
   B: Yes, I _____.

2. **A:** What _____ do you usually get up?
   B: I usually _____ _____ around 5:30, but I sometimes get up _____ 6:30.

3. **A:** _____ you leave home early in the morning?
   B: No, I _____. I usually _____ home at 8 o'clock.

4. **A:** _____ _____ do you usually start school?
   B: I always _____ at 9 o'clock.

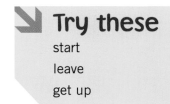

↘ **Try these**
start
leave
get up

C. **Pairs. Take turns asking and answering the questions above, using true information.**

3 LISTEN AND UNDERSTAND

 Track 26 **A.** Debbie is talking about her weekly schedule. Listen and write the times.

	Weekdays	Weekends
1. get up		
2. have breakfast		
3. go to bed		

B. Listen again. How many times does she go to yoga class every week? _____

4 JOIN IN

A. Groups. Fill in the chart about yourself. Then talk to two other people.

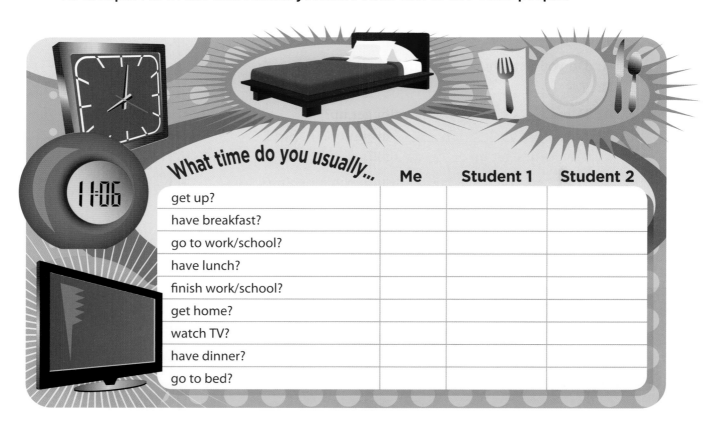

What time do you usually...	Me	Student 1	Student 2
get up?			
have breakfast?			
go to work/school?			
have lunch?			
finish work/school?			
get home?			
watch TV?			
have dinner?			
go to bed?			

B. Groups. Find a good time for you and the people you spoke to in A to...

meet for lunch   see a movie together

1 THINGS TO DO

CD 1 Track 27 **A. What do you like to do in your free time? Circle the things you like. Then listen and repeat.**

1. a fashion show

2. a barbecue

3. a soccer game

4. an IT fair

5. a movie

6. a theme park

7. a science museum

8. a dance club

9. a rock concert

B. Pairs. Compare your answers from A with a partner. How many places do you both like to go?

A: I like fashion shows.

B: So do I. / Oh, I don't.

A: I don't like fashion shows.

B: Neither do I. / Oh, I do.

C. Groups. Talk to your classmates and find two things you both like to do and two things you both don't like to do. Then tell the rest of the class.

> Keiko and I both like fashion shows and dance clubs. We don't like...

2 CONVERSATION STRATEGY: ACCEPTING AND DECLINING INVITATIONS

 Track 28 **A. Pairs. Listen to the conversations. Then practice with a partner.**

1. **A:** Are you free on Saturday afternoon?
   B: Yes. I'm not doing anything.
   A: Would you like to see a fashion show?
   B: A fashion show? *Sure, that sounds fun.*

2. **A:** Would you like to do something on Friday night?
   B: *Oh, sorry. I can't.* I'm working late.
   A: How about Saturday night? Would you like to go to a dance club?
   B: *Sure, that would be great.*

B. Notice how we accept or decline invitations. We can also use these expressions:

Accept:	**Decline:**
Sure.	*(Oh,) Sorry, I can't.*
Thanks. That would be great.	*I'm afraid I'm not free.*
Yeah, I'd love to…	*I'd like to, but I can't.*

Pairs. Now practice the conversations in A again, using different expressions to accept or decline.

C. Pairs. Use expressions from B to accept or decline these invitations. Then practice with a partner and add information of your own.

1. **A:** Would you like to go to a theme park on Saturday?
   B: _____ (*decline*)

   A: OK. How about Sunday then?
   B: _____ (*accept*)

2. **A:** Hey, would you like to see a movie tonight?
   B: _____ (*decline*)

   A: All right. What about tomorrow night?
   B: _____ (*accept*)

D. Pairs. Practice the conversations from A again. This time use your own information.

3 LISTEN AND UNDERSTAND

CD 1 Track 29

A. Listen to people inviting friends to do things. Where do they invite their friends? Number four of the items from 1 to 4 in the order you hear them.

___ a science museum   ___ an IT fair   ___ a barbecue

___ a fashion show   ___ a rock concert   ___ a soccer game

B. Listen again. Does their friend accept or decline? Check (✓) the correct column.

1. ☐ accept   ☐ decline   3. ☐ accept   ☐ decline
2. ☐ accept   ☐ decline   4. ☐ accept   ☐ decline

4 JOIN IN

A. Think of four things you would like to invite your classmates to do with you. Write them in the chart as in the example.

Event	Name	Accept	Decline
Go to a Pilates class tonight	Michelle	no	has a date

B. Class activity. Invite three classmates to do the activities you wrote in A. Do they accept or decline? If they decline, write the reason in the box.

Food and Meals

LESSON 1: Likes and dislikes

1 SNACKS

A. Are these snacks or drinks? Write *S* for snack and *D* for drink.

_____ cookie

_____ soda

_____ nuts

_____ tea

_____ fruit

_____ milk

CD 1 Track 30 **B.** Pairs. Listen to the conversation. Then practice with a partner.

A: 1 Do you want something to drink?

B: Yes, please.

A: How about a coffee?

B: No, thanks. 2 I don't drink much coffee. Do you have any soda?

A: Sure. And how about something to eat? 3 Maybe some cookies?

B: Oh, yes, please.

C. Pairs. Practice the conversation again. Use this information.

Practice 1

1 Would you like something to drink?

2 I never drink coffee.

3 Do you want some fruit?

Practice 2

1 Can I get you something to drink?

2 I never drink coffee at night.

3 Do you want some nuts?

D. Class activity. Ask four classmates which of the snacks and drinks in A they've had in the past two days. Can you think of other snacks and drinks to ask about? Tell the rest of the class what you learned.

2 LANGUAGE FOCUS: COUNT AND NON-COUNT NOUNS

 Track 31 **A.** Listen and practice.

Count	
I like *tomatoes*.	
I don't like *carrots*.	
I don't like them at all.	
Do you eat *many cookies?*	Yes, I eat a lot.
	No, I don't eat *many/any*.
oranges, nuts, bananas, vegetables, mangoes, strawberries	

Non-count	
I like *rice*.	
I don't like *broccoli*.	
I don't like it very much.	
Do you drink *much coffee?*	Yes, I drink a lot.
	No, I don't drink *much/any*.
milk, cheese, bread, tea, yogurt, meat, fruit	

 Track 32 **B. Pairs. Complete the conversations with items from A. Listen and check your answers. Then practice with a partner.**

1. **A:** What fruit do you like? Do you like bananas?
   B: Yes, I do. I like _____ a lot.

2. **A:** Do you eat _____ vegetables?
   B: Yes, I eat _____ vegetables. I love carrots.

3. **A:** Do you eat _____ nuts?
   B: No, I _____ eat many.

4. **A:** Do you eat _____ broccoli?
   B: Yes, I do. I like it a _____.

5. **A:** Do you drink _____ tea?
   B: No, I don't drink _____ tea. I don't really like it.

6. **A:** I love fruit. I eat a lot of it. What about you?
   B: Yeah, I love _____ too. My favorites are mangoes and strawberries.

7. **A:** Do you have coffee for breakfast?
   B: No, I don't drink _____ coffee in the morning, but I drink a lot during the day.

8. **A:** Do you eat _____ meat?
   B: No, I don't eat _____. But I eat a lot of cheese and yogurt.

C. Pairs. Take turns asking and answering the questions above, using true information.

Unit 4   **25**

3 LISTEN AND UNDERSTAND

A. **Peter and Mary are preparing a shopping list for the supermarket. Listen and check (✓) the things they are going to buy.**

	Going to buy	Not liked	Not needed
1. broccoli			
2. noodles			
3. chocolate			
4. milk			
5. carrots			
6. mangoes			
7. cheese			

B. **Listen again. For the things they *don't* plan to buy, check (✓) the reason.**

4 JOIN IN

A. **Class activity. Ask your classmates questions about the things below. Write one person's name next to each item.**

Find someone who...

doesn't like green tea ice cream _____

has a big breakfast _____

drinks a lot of coffee _____

doesn't eat meat _____

eats a lot of fruit _____

doesn't like carrots _____

eats a lot of take-out food _____

likes yogurt a lot _____

eats a lot of hamburgers _____

doesn't eat a lot of rice _____

eats a lot of chocolate _____

doesn't like noodles _____

B. **Pairs. Discuss what you found out in A with a partner.**

1 AT A RESTAURANT

 Track 34 **A.** **What kind of food is it? Write *A* for appetizer, *M* for main course, *D* for dessert, or *B* for beverage. Then listen and check your answers.**

fish with fried rice

steak with french fries

ice cream

tomato soup

apple pie

grilled chicken with vegetables

soda

salad

tea

B. **Pairs. Circle one thing you like from each row in A. Then discuss your answers with a partner.**

A: I like ice cream a lot.
B: I like it too, but I like apple pie better.

C. **Pairs. What are three foods you like? What are three foods you don't like? Compare with a partner.**

A: I like mangoes, mushrooms, and any kind of soup. How about you?
B: Well, I like mushrooms too. But I really don't care for mangoes, and I only like hot and sour soup.
A: Oh! Hot and sour soup is my favorite. Why don't you like other soups?

2 CONVERSATION STRATEGY: CONFIRMING INFORMATION

A. Pairs. Listen to the conversations. Then practice with a partner.

1. **A:** Are you ready to order?
   B: Yes, I'd like a green salad, grilled chicken with vegetables, and tea.
   A: OK. *So that's a green salad, grilled chicken with vegetables, and tea.*
   B: That's right.

2. **A:** Would you like anything else?
   B: Yes, I'll have a coffee with cream, but no dessert.
   A: *Did you say coffee with cream and dessert?*
   B: No, coffee with cream, but no dessert.

B. Notice how we confirm information by repeating a phrase or by asking for clarification.

By repeating:
A: *Can I get you a drink?*

B: *Yes, I'll take a soda water please.*

A: *So that's a soda water for you?*

B: *That's right.*

By clarifying:
A: *And for your main course?*

B: *I'll have steak and french fries with a green salad.*

A: *Did you say steak and french fries with a green salad?*

B: *Yes, please.*

Pairs. Now practice the conversations in A again, using different expressions to confirm information.

C. Pairs. Confirm these orders by repeating or clarifying. Then practice with a partner and add other information if you can.

1. **A:** Are you ready to order?
   B: Yes, I'll have tomato soup, spaghetti, and apple pie, please.
   A: So _____.

2. **A:** Can I get you a starter?
   B: Yes. I'd like vegetable soup, and my friend will have a green salad.
   A: Did you _____?

D. Pairs. Practice the conversations in A again. This time use your own information.

3 LISTEN AND UNDERSTAND

Track 36 **A. Listen to a customer ordering in a restaurant. Circle her order.**

Appetizers	Main courses	Beverages	Desserts
broccoli soup	fried chicken	milkshake	fried bananas
mango salad	grilled fish	fresh juice	strawberries
tomato salad	pepper steak	soda	ice cream

B. Listen again. Does the server take the order correctly? _____ Yes _____ No

4 JOIN IN

A. Look at the menu and decide what you want to order.

Appetizers
Soup of the day	$4.95
Vegetable platter	$9.50

Main Courses
Fish of the day	$12.95
Steak	$17.95
Baked chicken	$15.00

Side Dishes
Tomato salad	$6.00
Green salad	$4.50

Desserts
Cake	$4.95
Cookies	$3.00

Beverages
Bottled water	$2.50
Soda pop	$1.95
Milk	$1.50

B. Role play. Take turns being the customer and the server, and order a meal from the menu above. (You can use some of the questions below as you talk with your partner.)

Try these

Are you ready to order?
Would you like an appetizer?
What are you having for your main course?
Are you having dessert?
What would you like to drink?

LESSON 1: Finding out what people do

1 WHAT DO YOU DO?

A. Number the pictures below.

1. languages   **2.** business   **3.** software design   **4.** fashion design

CD 1 Track 37 **B. Pairs. Listen to the conversation. Then practice with a partner.**

A: What do you do? Are you a student?

B: 1 Yes, I am.

A: Where do you go to school?

B: 2 I go to City College.

A: Really? And what are you studying there? Music?

B: 3 No, I'm studying Chinese.

A: That's interesting.

C. Pairs. Practice the conversation again. Use this information.

Practice 1

1 That's right.

2 I'm studying at Fairview Technical College.

3 No, I'm getting a business degree.

Practice 2

1 Yes, I'm still studying.

2 At a technical school.

3 No, I'm taking a fashion design course.

2 LANGUAGE FOCUS: *WH-* QUESTIONS

Track 38 **A. Listen and practice.**

What do you do?	I'm a *student / gym instructor*.
	I work in *a hotel*.
Where do you work?	I work in *a hotel*.
	I work for *City Bank*.
Where do you go to school?	I go to *City College*.
What are you studying?	I'm studying *business*.
Where do you live?	I live *downtown*.
When do you finish your course?	I graduate *next year*.

Track 39 **B. Pairs. Complete the conversations with items from A. Listen and check your answers. Then practice with a partner.**

1. **A:** What _____ you do, Kazu?
   B: I'm a student at City College.
   A: And _____ do you live?
   B: On campus.
   A: Cool.

2. **A:** What do you _____, Maria?
   B: I work for a software company.
   A: Really? And what _____ you _____ there?
   B: I design software.
   A: Wow.

3. **A:** Tim, where do you _____ to school?
   B: I go to a technical college.
   A: And what _____ you studying?
   B: I'm taking a computer course.
   A: That's interesting.

C. Pairs. Take turns asking and answering the questions above, using true information.

3 LISTEN AND UNDERSTAND

A. Listen to people talking about what they do. Correct the information by crossing out what's wrong and write the correct information in the last column.

Tony	teacher	East-West College	subject: music	
Amy	salesperson	Galaxy Department Store	section: children's	
Tracy	high school student	International Academy	year: 1	

B. Listen again. How does each person like his or her course or job?

	Likes it a lot	Doesn't like it very much
1. Tony	☐	☐
2. Amy	☐	☐
3. Tracy	☐	☐

4 JOIN IN

A. Pairs. You are helping correct these records. Ask your partner about the missing information and write it below. Student A: use this page. Student B: turn to page 78. Student B begins.

1.
Name: Margaret Long
Occupation: _____
Employer: _____
Address: 27 Spring Street, Bayview

2.
Name: _____
Occupation: student
School: New World College
Major: _____
Address: _____

Hi. What's your name?

What do you do?

My name's _____

I _____

B. Pairs. Now practice conversations like the ones in A, using true information about yourself.

1 JOBS

 Track 41 **A. Do you know people who do these jobs? Circle the people you know. Then listen and repeat.**

1. rock musician

2. computer programmer

3. tour guide

4. vet

5. flight attendant

6. hotel clerk

7. travel agent

8. security guard

9. DJ

B. Pairs. Which jobs do these phrases describe? (More than one answer is possible.) Talk with a partner and compare answers.

A: *Who gets free travel?*
B: *A flight attendant gets free travel.*
A: *And a flight attendant also wears a uniform.*
B: *You're right. And so does a tour guide.*

↘ Try these

gets free travel
works long hours
uses English at work
wears a uniform
works on weekends

C. Pairs. What job would you like? Talk to your partner.

2 CONVERSATION STRATEGY: AGREEING AND DISAGREEING

 Track 42 **A.** **Pairs. Listen to the conversations. Then practice with a partner.**

1. **A:** You know, I'd really like to be a tour guide.
   B: Really?
   A: Yes, I think it sounds so interesting.
   B: *Oh, I don't think so.*

2. **A:** I think I'd like to be a computer programmer.
   B: Why?
   A: I think it sounds fun.
   B: *Yeah, I think so too.*

B. **Notice how we agree or disagree with people's opinions.**

You agree:	**You're not sure:**	**You disagree:**
Oh, me too.	*Really?*	*Oh, I don't think so.*
Yes, I think so too.	*I'm not sure.*	*I disagree. I think _____*
		I don't think so.

Pairs. Now practice the conversations in A again, using different expressions to agree and disagree.

C. **Pairs. Use items from B and the words below to agree or disagree with these opinions. Then practice with a partner and add information of your own.**

1. **A:** I'd love to be a DJ. It sounds cool.
   B: _____

2. **A:** I'd hate to be a police officer. It sounds difficult.
   B: _____

3. **A:** I'd like to be a gym instructor.
   B: _____

4. **A:** I'd love to be a vet. It sounds great.
   B: _____

> **Try these**
> interesting   difficult
> cool   easy
> fun   dangerous
> boring

D. **Pairs. Practice the conversations in A again. This time use your own information.**

3 LISTEN AND UNDERSTAND

 Track 43 **A.** **Listen to people talking about jobs. Number three of the jobs from 1 to 3 in the order you hear them.**

music teacher   singer   DJ   flight attendant

B. **Listen again. Does the person they are talking to agree or disagree?**

1. ☐ agrees   ☐ disagrees
2. ☐ agrees   ☐ disagrees
3. ☐ agrees   ☐ disagrees

4 JOIN IN

A. **Pairs. Think of three jobs for the following people.**

someone who likes to travel _____

someone who likes to meet people _____

someone who likes to work outdoors _____

someone who likes selling things _____

B. **Pairs. Do the jobs you listed in A sound interesting to you? Choose two and discuss them with your partner.**

A: I think a flight attendant is an interesting job. You get to meet new people all the time.

B: Yeah, and you get to go to cool places too.

A: You know, that would be a great job!

B: Do you need a lot of training?

A: I don't know. We should do some research to find out.

LESSON 1: Where's the subway station?

1 ASKING FOR LOCATIONS

A. Number the pictures below.

1. taxi stand   3. ATM   5. food stall
2. Internet cafe   4. mailbox   6. subway station

 Track 44 **B. Pairs. Listen to the conversation. Then practice with a partner.**

A: Excuse me. 1 I'm looking for the subway station.

B: Sure. There's one just down the street on the left.

A: Oh, thanks. 2 And I also need to find an ATM.

B: Let me think. Oh yeah, there are some in the mall.

A: Thanks a lot.

B: 3 You're welcome.

C. Pairs. Practice the conversation again. Use this information.

Practice 1

1 I need to find a mailbox.

2 And where can I find an Internet cafe?

3 Sure.

Practice 2

1 I'm trying to find a taxi stand.

2 And where can I find a fast-food place?

3 No problem.

2 LANGUAGE FOCUS: *THERE IS / THERE ARE* + PREPOSITIONS OF PLACE

 Track 45 **A. Listen and practice.**

Where's the subway station?	*There's* one	*down* the street. *next to* the department store. *across from* the hotel. *on* the corner.
Where are the fast-food places?	*There are* some	*in* the mall. *near* the station. *on* King Street.

 Track 46 **B. Pairs. Complete the conversations with items from A and the map below. Listen and check your answers. Then practice with a partner.**

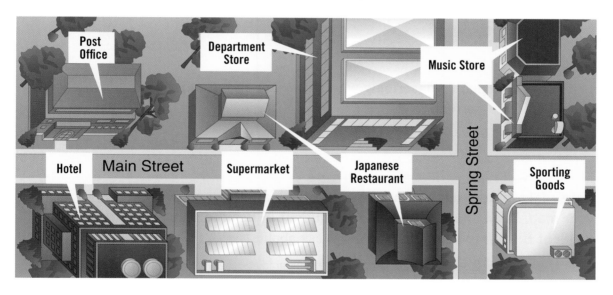

1. **A:** Excuse me, I'm trying to find a post office.
   B: Sure, there's one _____ _____ the hotel.

2. **A:** Where can I find a supermarket?
   B: A supermarket? Oh yes, there's _____ next to the _____.

3. **A:** Excuse me, I'm looking for a department store.
   B: Sure, there's one _____ _____ the music store.

4. **A:** Excuse me. I'm trying to find a Japanese restaurant.
   B: I think there are two _____ Main Street.

5. **A:** Hi. Where can I find a sporting goods store?
   B: There's one _____ the corner of Spring Street and Main Street.

6. **A:** Excuse me. I'm looking for a music store.
   B: A music store? Um, I think _____ _____ some on Spring Street.

C. Pairs. Take turns asking and answering the questions above, using true information.

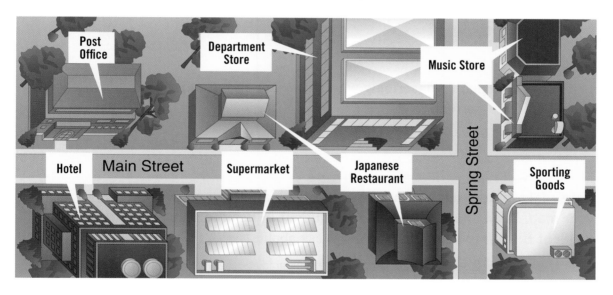 is the map showing:
Post Office, Department Store, Music Store, Hotel, Main Street, Supermarket, Japanese Restaurant, Spring Street, Sporting Goods

3 LISTEN AND UNDERSTAND

Track 47 **A. Listen to people asking about locations. Write them on the map.**

1. taxi stand   **2.** souvenir shops   **3.** movie theaters   **4.** bus stop

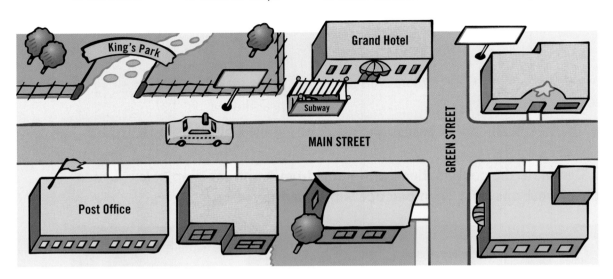

B. Listen again to people describing where they are and number their locations from 1 to 4 on the map in A.

4 JOIN IN

A. Pairs. Take turns asking about these locations and then mark them on your map. Then check your answers. Student A: use the picture below. Student B: turn to page 79. Student A ask about:

1. an ATM   **2.** a drugstore   **3.** a supermarket   **4.** a camera shop

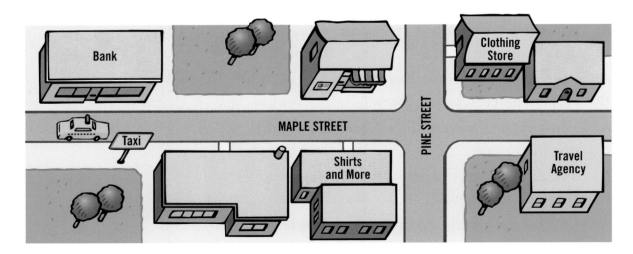

A: *Excuse me, I'm looking for _____.*
B: *There _____ on the corner of Pine Street and Maple Street.*
A: *Thanks very much.*
B: *You're welcome.*

1 LANDMARKS

  Track 48

A. (Circle) the things that are in your town. Then listen and repeat.

1. a bridge

2. a park

3. a temple

4. a statue

5. a fountain

6. a train station

7. an apartment building

8. a stadium

9. a museum

B. **Pairs. Write an X on the places in A that you would not like to have in your neighborhood. Then tell your partner what you think. Give as many details as possible.**

A: *I wouldn't like to have a train station near my house.*

B: *Really? Why not?*

A: *I think it would be too loud. And there would be too many people around.*

C. **Groups. Where do you live? What landmarks are near your home? Compare with others.**

A: *I live downtown. I live in an apartment building. There's a park down the street.*

B: *I live near the university. There's a stadium across from our apartment building. There aren't any parks around.*

A. Pairs. Listen to the conversations. Then practice with a partner.

1. **A:** How do I get to your place?

   B: Take bus number 114 and get off at the high school. Then turn right and walk along North Street. Our apartment is across from the bus stop.

   A: *Could you say that again, please?*

   B: Sure. Take bus number 114 and get off at the high school. Then you'll turn right and walk along North Street. You'll find our apartment across from the bus stop.

2. **A:** Can you tell me how to get to your office?

   B: Sure. Take the subway and get off at Lake Station. At the station, cross the bridge and turn left on Pine Street. The address is 116 Pine Street.

   A: *Let me repeat that.* So, I take the subway and get off at Lake Station. At the station, I cross the bridge and turn left on Pine Street. Your address is 116 Pine Street.

   B: That's right.

B. Notice how we check information by asking for repetition or saying we'll repeat something.

Would you mind saying that again, please?   *Let me check that I got that right.*

Pairs. Now practice the conversations in A again, using different expressions to check information.

C. Pairs. Use words from B to check information in these conversations. Then practice with a partner and add information of your own.

1. **A:** I need to get to the museum. Do you know how to get there?

   B: Sure. Just hop on the A train and go three stops. It's right there.

   A: _____

   B: You're right, but go just three stops instead of four.

   A: OK. Thanks for your help.

2. **A:** I heard there's a great fountain downtown. Is it near the bridge?

   B: No, it's actually closer to the park, near the statue.

   A: _____

   B: Sure. It's close to the park, near the statue.

   A: Great. Do you want to come check it out with me?

D. Pairs. Practice the conversations from A again. This time use your own information.

3 LISTEN AND UNDERSTAND

 Track 50 **A. Listen to people inviting friends to visit them. Complete the information below.**

	When	Address	How to get there	Nearest landmark
1.		4/22 West St.		museum
2.		7/19 Market Street		
3.				

B. Listen again and check (✓) if these statements are True or False.

	True	False
1. He lives in a new apartment building.	☐	☐
2. You can walk to his house from the station.	☐	☐
3. Their place is next to the station.	☐	☐

4 JOIN IN

A. Role play. Have a conversation with your partner.

1. Invite your partner to go out with you this weekend.
2. Suggest a place to meet, for example, a movie theater, a cafe, or a restaurant.
3. Your partner is not sure where it is. Say what place it is near.

A: Let's do something on Saturday night.

B: Sure. That sounds great.

A: Why don't we meet at Toby's Cafe on King Street?

B: Where exactly is that?

A: It's just past the Central Department Store. There's a theater nearby. Maybe we can eat and then watch a movie.

B: Sounds like fun.

LESSON 1: Homes and apartments

1 WHAT'S YOUR APARTMENT LIKE?

A. Number the picture.

1. elevator	**3.** dining room	**5.** bathroom	**7.** first floor	**9.** kitchen
2. balcony	**4.** bedroom	**6.** lobby	**8.** second floor	**10.** living room

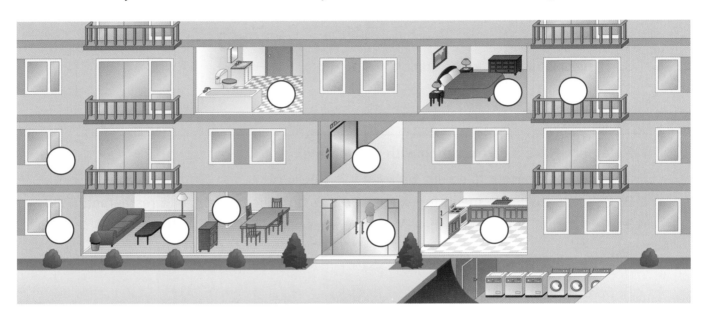

 Track 2 **B. Pairs. Listen to the conversation. Then practice with a partner.**

A: What's your new apartment like?

B: 1 It's nice. It's quite big.

A: Really? Does it have a view?

B: 2 Yes, it does. It has a city view.

A: I see. And is there parking?

B: 3 Yes, there's parking in the basement.

A: Well, that sounds really nice. I hope you enjoy living there.

B: Me too.

C. Pairs. Practice the conversation again. Use this information.

Practice 1

1 It's good, and it's quiet.

2 Not really. It's on the ground floor.

3 Yes, there's a parking space in front.

Practice 2

1 It's good, and it's not far from my school.

2 Yes, it looks over a park.

3 No, we have to park on the street.

2 LANGUAGE FOCUS: QUESTIONS WITH *IS THERE* AND *DOES*

A. Listen and practice.

Is there	a view?	Yes, there is.
	a yard?	No, there isn't.
Does it have	a balcony?	Yes, it does.
	an elevator?	No, doesn't.
Does it have	a dining room?	Yes, it does.
Is there	a dining room?	Yes, there is.
It doesn't have an elevator.		It has a dining room.
There isn't a swimming pool.		There is a balcony.

B. Complete the conversations with items from A. Listen and check your answers. Then practice with a partner.

1. **A:** What's your apartment like?
   B: It's really great. It's quite big.
   A: _____ it have a view?
   B: Yes, it does. It _____ a view of the park.
   A: Nice. Is _____ a balcony?
   B: No, there _____.
   A: That's too bad. Does it _____ a dining room?
   B: Yes, it does.
   A: Great. And _____ a game room?
   B: A game room? No, _____.
   A: Oh, that would be nice.

2. **A:** What's your new apartment like?
   B: It's fantastic. I really love it.
   A: How many bedrooms _____ it have?
   B: Two. It has two bedrooms and two bathrooms.
   A: That's great. _____ it have a balcony?
   B: Yes, it _____ There's a balcony near the living room.
   A: And _____ there a view from the balcony?
   B: No, _____ isn't.
   A: And what about a swimming pool? _____ a pool in the building?
   B: Yes, _____ I can go swimming every day.
   A: Nice.

C. Pairs. Take turns asking and answering the questions above, using true information.

A. Listen to people talking about their apartments and number three of the pictures from 1 to 3 in the order you hear about them.

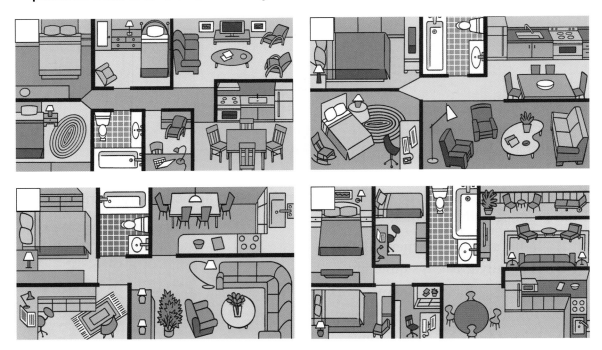

B. Listen again. Check (✓) what each person likes about his or her apartment.

1. _____ He has his own bedroom.   _____ He has his own bathroom.

2. _____ There's a study.   _____ There's a big kitchen.

3. _____ He likes the kitchen.   _____ The apartment has two bedrooms.

4 JOIN IN

A. Pairs. Compare your pictures. How many differences are there between the two apartments? Take turns asking your partner about his or her picture. Student A: use the picture below. Student B: turn to page 80.

Does your apartment have three bedrooms?
Is there a dining room and a living room?
Does it have a balcony?

B. Groups. Tell the people in your group about your home.

1 HOME ACTIVITIES

Track 6

A. Imagine you are a homestay guest. (Circle) the activities you think are acceptable for a homestay guest to do. Then listen and repeat.

1. use the kitchen

2. have friends over

3. watch TV

4. use the telephone

5. come home late

6. play loud music

7. use the washing machine

8. use the family computer

9. help wash the dishes

B. Pairs. What are some other things that are acceptable and not acceptable for a homestay guest to do? Talk with a partner.

A: Do you think it's OK to use the family car?

B: I guess so. / No, I don't think so.

C. Class activity. Talk to your classmates and ask if any of them have been on a homestay. Which activities did they do, and which did they think were not OK to do?

A. Pairs. Listen to the conversations. Then practice with a partner.

1. **A:** Is it OK if I use the telephone?
   B: Yes, that's fine.
   A: Thank you.

2. **A:** Do you mind if I watch TV?
   B: Sorry, not right now please. I'm reading.
   A: Sure. No problem.

B. Notice how we request permission and then accept or decline the request.

Requesting:	Accepting:	Declining:
Can I use the computer?	*Sure.*	*Sorry, not right now.*
Is it all right if I watch TV?	*Certainly.*	*Maybe later.*
	Yes, that's OK.	*Some other time maybe.*

Pairs. Now practice the conversations in A again, using different expressions to request permission and accept/decline.

C. Pairs. Use words from B to request permission and accept/decline. Then practice with a partner and add information of your own.

1. **A:** _____ I have friends over?
   B: Certainly.
   A: Super. We'll be in the living room studying.

2. **A:** Is it _____ if I come home late?
   B: _____, not tonight.
   A: OK. I'll be home by 8 then.

3. **A:** Do you _____ _____ I use the washing machine?
   B: _____, that's OK.
   A: Thanks. I appreciate it.

4. **A:** Is _____ _____ if I help with washing dishes?
   B: Certainly!
   A: OK. Where do I start?

D. Pairs. Practice the conversations in A again. This time use your own information.

> Is it OK if I have some friends over on Sunday afternoon?

> Can I use the computer to check my e-mail?

Track 8

A. Listen to guests asking for permission to do things. Number the things they ask about from 1 to 6 in the order you hear them.

B. Listen again. Circle the picture in A if the person accepts the requests. Write an X on the picture if the person declines the request.

4 JOIN IN

A. Role play. Take turns. Student A: use the information below. Student B: turn to page 81.

Role play 1

You are a houseguest. Here are some things you would like to do. Add two more things to the list. Ask your host for permission.

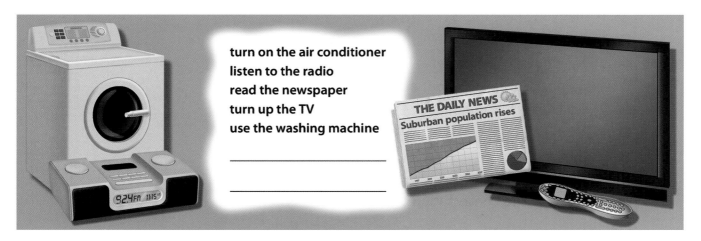

turn on the air conditioner
listen to the radio
read the newspaper
turn up the TV
use the washing machine

_____

_____

THE DAILY NEWS
Suburban population rises

Role play 2

You are a host. Your houseguest asks your permission to do things in your house. Accept or decline the requests. If you decline, give a reason.

LESSON 1: Keeping in touch

1 HEY, THAT'S COOL!

A. Pairs. Number the pictures below. How many of these things do you have with you today? Tell your partner.

1. digital camera
2. MP3 player
3. electronic dictionary
4. scanner
5. cell phone
6. camcorder

a. _____

c. _____

e. _____

b. _____

d. _____

f. _____

CD 2 Track 9 **B.** Pairs. Listen to the conversation. Then practice with a partner.

A: Is that your new digital camera?

B: Yes. I love it.

A: 1 Do you use it very often?

B: Yes, I do. I use it just about every day.

A: 2 What do you use it for?

B: 3 Oh, I like to take pictures of my friends. Take a look.

A: Yeah. That's cool.

C. Pairs. Practice the conversation again. Use this information.

Practice 1

1 Do you use it a lot?

2 What do you do with it?

3 I take pictures of my dog.

Practice 2

1 Do you use it much?

2 What for?

3 Oh, I like to send pictures to my parents.

2 **LANGUAGE FOCUS: ADVERB PHRASES**

 A. **Listen and practice.**

How often do you use your camera?	I use it *all the time.*
Do you use your camera very often?	I use it *pretty often / a lot.*
Do you use it a lot?	I use it *from time to time.*
	I don't use it *very often.*
	I *hardly ever* use it.
	I *never* use it.

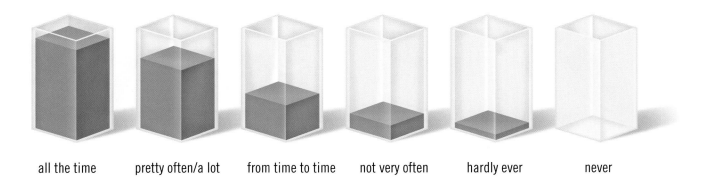

all the time   pretty often/a lot   from time to time   not very often   hardly ever   never

 Track 11 **B.** **Pairs. Complete the conversations with items from A and the words below. Listen and check your answers. (Different answers are possible.) Then practice with a partner.**

1. **A:** Hey, Yu-ting. Do you have a digital camera?
   B: Yes, I do.
   A: I guess you use it a lot.
   B: No, not really. I don't use it very often actually.
   A: So what do you use it for then?
   B: _____

2. **A:** Do you have an MP3 player, Tom?
   B: Yeah, I just bought a new one last month. It's cool.
   A: How often do you use it?
   B: _____

3. **A:** Do you have an electronic dictionary?
   B: Yes, I got one last year.
   A: Do you use it a lot?
   B: _____
   A: Really? For learning English, you mean?
   B: Yes, I check new English words from time to time. It's easy to use.

Try these
Yeah. Pretty often.
No, I hardly ever use it.
Oh, I use it all the time.
I use it from time to time for school projects.

C. **Pairs. Practice the conversations above, using true information.**

CD 2 Track 12 **A.** Listen to people talking about things they own. Number the things they are talking about from 1 to 6 in the order you hear them.

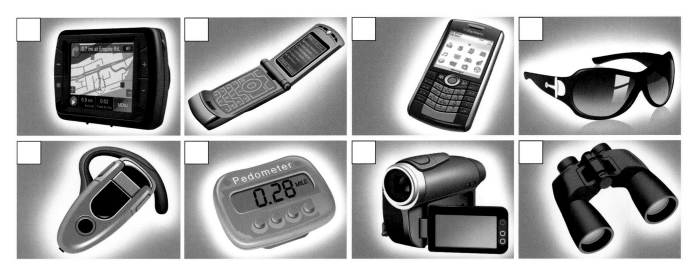

B. Listen again. Do they use the things a lot or hardly ever?

	1	2	3	4	5	6
A lot						
Hardly ever						

4 JOIN IN

A. Make a list of items you use a lot and a list of items you use from time to time.

B. Pairs. Talk with your partner. Do you have any of the same things on your list from A? Ask follow-up questions to find out more about the things your partner uses.

A: Do you ever use the Internet?

B: Well, I use it from time to time. How about you?

A: Yeah, I use it a lot. I look up things for class, send e-mails...

1 INTERESTING PRODUCTS

 A. Look at these products. Check (✓) the ones you would buy. Then listen and repeat.

1. electric skateboard

2. backpack with wheels

3. neon sunglasses

4. electric bike

5. hybrid vehicle

6. cordless wave keyboard

7. flexible camera tripod

8. motorized scuba bike

B. Pairs. Discuss your answers from A with a partner.

A: I'd like to have an electric skateboard. It's looks kind of fun.

B: Yeah. Me too. But, I don't think I'd want neon sunglasses. They're not very useful.

A: I agree. Would you buy a scuba bike?

B: Sure. Why not?

A: I don't think I would.

C. Groups. Tell your group what other cool things you'd like to buy and why you'd like to buy them.

Track 14 **A. Pairs. Listen to the conversations. Then practice with a partner.**

1. **A:** What's that?

   B: It's my new digital camera.

   A: *It's neat.* Can I take a look at it?

   B: Sure.

   A: Wow. *That's amazing.*

2. **A:** How do you like my new cell phone?

   B: Let me take a look.

   A: Sure. Here you are.

   B: *It's awesome.*

3. **A:** What do you think of my new skateboard?

   B: Wow. Is it electric?

   A: Yes. It can go up to 20 kilometers per hour.

   B: *That's really cool.*

B. Notice how we can use various expressions to express enthusiasm about something:

That's cool.   It's awesome.   That's neat.   That looks amazing.   That's terrific.

Pairs. Now practice the conversations in A again, using different expressions to show interest.

C. Pairs. Use words from B to express enthusiasm in these conversations. Then practice with a partner and add information of your own.

1. **A:** What do you think about Ben's new keyboard?

   B: The cordless wave keyboard? It's _____!

   A: Yeah, I'm thinking about getting one too.

2. **A:** I think I'm going to get my mom a motorized scuba bike for her birthday.

   B: _____ terrific!

   A: She'll have a lot of fun using it when we go on vacation.

3. **A:** Did you see that backpack with wheels?

   B: No, I didn't. Was it cool?

   A: Yeah, it was really _____.

D. Class activity. Do your classmates have some cool things with them today? Talk about them together.

3 LISTEN AND UNDERSTAND

 Track 15 **A. People are looking at things in a store. Listen and check (✓) the things they are going to buy.**

   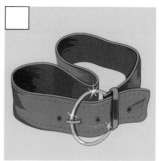

B. Listen again. Why did they decide to buy or not buy each item?

	1	2	3	4
Its look				
Its usefulness				

4 JOIN IN

A. Pairs. What do you think of these things? Use the language below and add ideas of your own to practice conversations with a partner.

A: *Do you like that bracelet?*
B: *I think it's kind of neat.*
A: *Really? I think it's weird.*

B: *What do you think of those earrings?*
A: *I think they're awesome.*
B: *Yeah, me too. They're really cool.*

It's a bit weird.

It's neat.

They're cool.

They're strange.

It's not useful.

Enjoying the Outdoors

LESSON 1: Seasonal activities

1 DO YOU EVER GO WATER-SKIING?

A. Number the pictures below. (Circle) the activities that you like to do.

1. swimming   **3.** rock climbing   **5.** canoeing
2. water-skiing   **4.** ice-skating   **6.** jogging

CD 2 Track 16 B. Pairs. Listen to the conversation. Then practice with a partner.

A: 1 Do you like swimming?
B: Yes, I like it a lot.
A: Me too. 2 How about water-skiing? Do you ever go water-skiing?
B: No, I don't. But I'd love to try it. It looks fun.
A: 3 Yeah, it does.

C. Pairs. Practice the conversation again. Use this information.

Practice 1
1 Do you enjoy ice-skating?
2 What about rock climbing? Do you ever go rock climbing?
3 I guess so, but it also looks a little scary.

Practice 2
1 Do you ever go canoeing?
2 What about white-water rafting? Do you ever go rafting?
3 Yes, it's awesome.

Track 17 **A. Listen and practice.**

I	love	swimming.
	enjoy	camping.
	like	white-water rafting.
	don't mind	canoeing.
	don't like	skiing.
	can't stand	sailing.
	hate	snow-boarding.

Track 18 **B. Pairs. Match each question with its response. Then ask and answer the questions with a partner.**

1. Do you like swimming in the ocean?
2. Do you enjoy camping?
3. Do you like white-water rafting?
4. Do you like jogging?
5. Do you enjoy canoeing?
6. Do you like skiing?

a. Oh, no. It's too cold.
b. Yes, I do. it's really exciting.
c. No, I don't like sleeping outdoors.
d. Not really. I prefer walking slowly.
e. Yes, I do. It's really relaxing.
f. No, I don't. I prefer swimming in a pool.

C. Groups. How do you keep fit? What weekend activities do you enjoy? Discuss your answers with your group.

A: How do you keep fit?

B: Well, I like jogging and I also...

D. Pairs. Practice the questions in B again, using true information.

A. Listen to people talking about outdoor activities. Number the activities they talk about from 1 to 4 in the order you hear them.

B. Listen again. What do they think about each activity? (More than one answer is possible.)

	Exciting	Difficult	Fun	Dangerous	Expensive	Relaxing
1.						
2.						
3.						
4.						

4   JOIN IN

A. Groups. Write the names of four outdoor activities in the chart. Then talk to three classmates and find out how they feel about doing the things on your list.

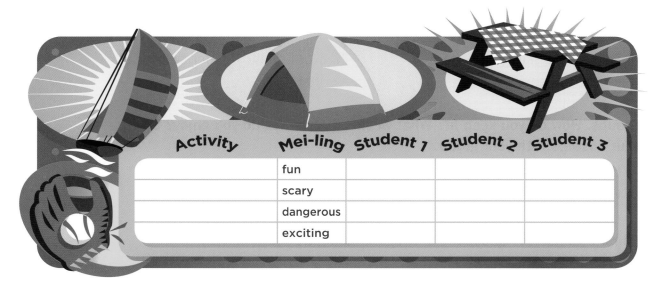

Activity	Mei-ling	Student 1	Student 2	Student 3
	fun			
	scary			
	dangerous			
	exciting			

LESSON 2: Weekend activities

1 WAYS TO RELAX OR KEEP FIT

 Track 20 **A.** Check (✓) the things that you do. (Circle) the things you would like to try. Then listen and repeat.

1. jogging

2. hiking

3. skate-boarding

4. walking

5. mountain biking

6. snorkeling

7. bicycling

8. bodysurfing

9. horseback riding

B. Pairs. Discuss your answers from A with your partner.

A: *Do you ever go jogging?*
B: *Sometimes. Do you?*
A: *No, I don't.*

A: *Do you ever go snorkeling?*
B: *Snorkeling? No, but I'd like to try it sometime.*
A: *Me too.*

C. Pairs. What other things do you do to relax or keep fit? Make a list and discuss it with your partner.

2 CONVERSATION STRATEGY: USING ECHO QUESTIONS

 Track 21 **A. Pairs. Listen to the conversations. Then practice with a partner.**

1. **A:** Where's a good place to go snorkeling?
   B: *Snorkeling?* I'm not sure you can go snorkeling around here.
   A: I see. Well, can you go bodysurfing here at all?
   B: *Bodysurfing?* Yes, I think you can do that at the water park.

2. **A:** Where's a good place around here to go jogging?
   B: *Jogging?* You can go jogging in New Park.
   A: OK. And I'd like to do some bicycling too this weekend.
   B: *Bicycling?* Sure, you can do that in the park too.

B. Notice how we sometimes give ourselves more time to think, by using echo questions:

Bicycling?   Bodysurfing?   Snorkeling?   Jogging?

Pairs. Now practice the conversations in A again, using different activities and echo questions.

C. Pairs. Add echo questions like the ones above to these conversations. Then practice with a partner and add information of your own.

1. **A:** Where can you go mountain biking around here?
   B: _____? Lots of people go mountain biking in the state park.
   A: OK. Thanks.

2. **A:** I'd love to try rock climbing. Do you know where I can go?
   B: _____? Sure. There's a place at my college.
   A: Great. Thanks.

3. **A:** Have you ever tried ice hockey, Mark?
   B: _____? Once or twice when I was at college. It was fun.
   A: Yeah. It's a great sport.

4. **A:** What's the most popular summer sport in your country, Kazu?
   B: _____? Baseball, I guess. People really love it.
   A: Oh, yeah. I've seen it on TV.

D. Practice the conversations from A again. This time use your own information.

3 LISTEN AND UNDERSTAND

A. People are talking about things you can do in places in their city. Check (✓) the things they can do in each place.

	Swimming	Skateboarding	Cycling	Horseback riding
botanical gardens				
university campus				
city park				

B. Listen again. When is a good time to go to each place? (More than one answer is possible.)

	Weekdays	Weekends	Public holidays
1.			
2.			
3.			
4.			

4 JOIN IN

A. Pairs. What are some unusual and interesting outdoor activities people can enjoy in your town or city? Complete the chart with a partner.

ACTIVITY	PLACES TO GO	BEST TIME TO GO

B. Groups. Discuss your ideas from A with others in your group.

LESSON 1: Prices

1 HOW MUCH IS IT?

A. Match the pictures and words. (Circle) any of the things you have bought lately.

1. CD player	**3.** TV	**5.** clock	**7.** laptop
2. DVD player	**4.** headphones	**6.** speaker	**8.** printer

CD 2 Track 23 **B. Pairs. Listen to the conversation. Then practice with a partner.**

A: 1 I like this CD player. How much is it, please?

B: Let me see. Yeah, it's $69.

A: 2 I see. That's not bad. And how much is this one?

B: Oh, that one is $145.

A: Wow. That's expensive.

B: Well, take a look at this one. It's not too expensive.

C. Pairs. Practice the conversation again. Use this information.

Practice 1

1 I'm interested in this watch. How much does it cost?

2 OK. And what about that one over there. How much is that one?

Practice 2

1 Can you show me that DVD player? How much is it?

2 That's pretty reasonable. What about that other one?

2 LANGUAGE FOCUS: QUESTIONS WITH *HOW MUCH*

 Track 24 **A. Listen and practice.**

How much is the digital camera?	It's $69.
How much does a CD player cost?	It costs about $170.
How much are these MP3 players?	They're $85.
How much do those DVD players cost?	They're $60.

Track 25 **B. Pairs. Complete the conversations with items from A and the words below. Listen and check your answers. Then practice with a partner.**

1. **A:** Excuse me. How much _____ this camera?
   B: This one? Let me see. Um… _____ $110.
   A: Wow. That's _____.

2. **A:** Good morning. Can I help you?
   B: How much _____ these CDs?
   A: These? Yes, they're all on special, sir. _____ all just $19.

3. **A:** Hi. How much _____ this TV cost?
   B: Oh, yes, that's a great TV. It only _____ $350.
   A: Mm. That's _____.

4. **A:** Excuse me. _____ are these headphones?
   B: Mmm. Let me check. _____ just $47.
   A: Thanks. I'll take them, please.

5. **A:** How much is this radio?
   B: This radio? It's _____, ma'am. _____ $180.
   A: That's not too bad actually.

6. **A:** Excuse me. How _____ these video games?
   B: Oh, _____ only $19.99 each this week.
   A: Thanks. I'll take these two, please.

Try these

very expensive	pretty cheap
quite expensive	cheap
reasonable	

C. Pairs. Practice the conversations again, using true information.

3 LISTEN AND UNDERSTAND

CD 2 Track 26 **A.** Koichi is talking to a travel agent about the price of things in Australia. Write down the price of each thing.

Koichi's Opinion				
Item	Price	Cheap	Reasonable	Expensive
a hamburger	$ – $			
a bus ride	$ – $			
a DVD	$ – $			
a movie ticket	$ – $			

B. Listen again. How does Koichi feel about the prices? Look at A and check (✓) his opinions.)

4 JOIN IN

A. Role play. Take turns. Student A: use the information below. Student B: turn to page 82.

Role play 1

You are an overseas traveler talking to a travel agent. You want to know about prices in the country you are going to visit. Add two more items to the list. Then ask the agent. Ask follow-up questions to find out more.

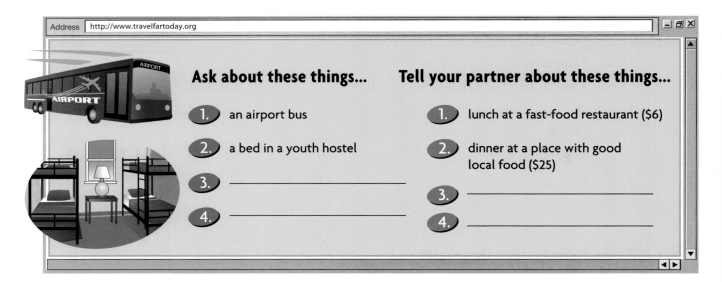

Address | http://www.travelfartoday.org

Ask about these things...
1. an airport bus
2. a bed in a youth hostel
3. _____
4. _____

Tell your partner about these things...
1. lunch at a fast-food restaurant ($6)
2. dinner at a place with good local food ($25)
3. _____
4. _____

A: How much is an airport bus?
B: I think it costs about $25.

Role play 2

You are a travel agent. An overseas traveler is asking you questions about prices in your country. Answer his or her questions.

1 **SHOPPING ITEMS**

 Track 27 **A.** **Look at the pictures. You want to buy these things. What kind of store could you go to for each item? Number the pictures. Then listen and repeat.**

1. bookstore   **3.** clothing store   **5.** electronic store   **7.** drugstore

2. sporting good store   **4.** supermarket   **6.** bakery   **8.** jewelry store

_____ flu medicine

_____ breakfast cereal

_____ watch

_____ sports shoes

_____ T-shirt

_____ sunglasses

_____ tennis balls

_____ lottery tickets

_____ magazines

_____ batteries

_____ cake

_____ pet food

B. **Pairs. Tell your partner where you would get each of the items from A.**

A: _You can get medicine at a drugstore._

B: _You can also get it at…_

C. **Pairs. Name two other things you can buy at each of the stores from A.**

> At a drugstore you can get shampoo and…

Track 28 **A.** **Pairs. Listen to the conversations. Then practice with a partner.**

1. **A:** I love this top. The design is really cool.
   B: *Yeah, I agree.*
   A: But I'm not sure about the color. I don't think it suits me.
   B: *Really? Why not?*

2. **A:** What do you think of this bag? I really like it.
   B: *I'm not sure.* It's very expensive.
   A: I guess it is, but it's a good brand.
   B: *I suppose so.*

B. **Notice how we can express agreement or disagreement with people's opinions.**

We agree:	**We don't really agree:**
I agree.	*Do you think so?*
You're right.	*I'm not sure.*
Yes, I think so too.	*I don't know about that.*
	I don't think so.

Pairs. Now practice the conversations in A again, using different expressions to react to opinions.

C. **Pairs. Use words from A and B to add reactions to these opinions. Then practice with a partner and add information of your own.**

1. **A:** Wow. Look at these jeans. I love the color.
   B: _____. It's a great color.

2. **A:** That's a really cool computer. But look at the price. It's so expensive.
   B: _____. They usually cost a lot more than that.

3. **A:** Hey, Michelle. Do you like this bracelet? I think it really looks good.
   B: Mm. _____. It really suits you.

4. **A:** That's a cute T-shirt. I really like it.
   B: _____. I think that one over there would suit you better.

5. **A:** Take a look at these basketball shoes, Sam. They're really weird.
   B: _____. I totally like them.

6. **A:** Wow. That's a good price for that MP3 player. It's a great brand.
   B: _____. I think you should buy it.

D. **Pairs. Practice the conversations in A again. This time use your own information.**

3 LISTEN AND UNDERSTAND

Track 29 **A.** Listen to people talking about things in a store. What does Maria think of them? Check (✓) the chart.

Item	Maria		Tony	
	likes	doesn't like	agrees	doesn't agree
bracelet				
sunglasses				
watch				
ring				

B. Listen again. Does Tony agree with Maria's opinions? Complete the chart.

4 JOIN IN

A. Class activity. Find three people in the class who have something cool/unusual/ interesting with them today. Complete the chart.

NAME	ITEM	YOUR REACTION
Kazu	sunglasses	cool design; awesome color

B. Groups. Discuss what you found out in B with your group.

A: I really like Kazu's sunglasses. The design is really cool and the color is awesome.

B: Yeah, I think so too.

unit 11 Tourism

LESSON 1: Things to see

1 WHAT DO YOU RECOMMEND?

A. Look at things visitors can do in Vietnam. Number the pictures below.

1. rent a bicycle
2. see a museum
3. see old buildings
4. take a tour
5. visit a market
6. buy handicrafts

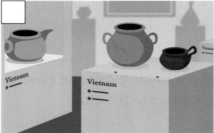

 Track 30 **B.** Pairs. Listen to the conversation. Then practice with a partner.

A: I'm going to Vietnam for the first time next month.

B: That's great. 1 It's a fascinating place.

A: 2 What places do you think I should visit?

B: You should go to Hanoi and Ho Chi Minh City.

A: What can you do in Hanoi?

B: Well, you should rent a bicycle and ride around the city. 3 It has some lovely old buildings.

A: It sounds great.

C. Pairs. Practice the conversation again. Use this information.

Practice 1	Practice 2
1 You'll really enjoy it.	1 I loved it when I was there.
2 What should I see?	2 Where should I go?
3 There are some lovely old streets in the city.	3 It has some good museums too.

66 Unit 11

Track 31 **A. Listen and practice.**

What *can* you do in Hanoi?	You *can* rent a bicycle.
	You *can* take a city tour.
Can you take a canal tour?	Yes, you *can*.
	No, you *can't*.
What *should* I do?	You *should* go to the museums.
What *should* I see?	You *should* see the Ho Chi Minh Memorial.
Should I take credit cards?	Yes, you *should*.
	No, you don't need to.

Track 32 **B. Match each question with its response. Then practice the conversations with a partner.**

1. What can a tourist do here?
2. What should you see?
3. Can you buy souvenirs downtown?
4. Do you think you should rent a car?
5. Where can you try local food?
6. Where can you get a good view of the city?

a. You should see the museum.
b. Well, you can take a city tour.
c. You can see everything from the TV tower.
d. You can go to the night market. They have local dishes.
e. No, you don't need to. It's not necessary.
f. Sure, you can buy some handicrafts there.

C. Pairs. Choose a city you and your partner know. Take turns asking and answering the questions above about the city you chose.

3 LISTEN AND UNDERSTAND

A. Listen to two people talking about places in a city. Check (✓) if the man recommends or doesn't recommends visiting these places.

	Recommends	Doesn't recommend	Reason
1. the market			
2. the old town			
3. the zoo			
4. the tower			

B. Listen again. Why does he recommend or not recommend the places? Write the reasons in the chart above.

4 JOIN IN

A. Complete the chart about three interesting cities to visit in your country. Write things you like (for example, the scenery, the climate, the location, the people, the food) and things you can do or see there (for example, go swimming, visit the science museum, visit a theme park).

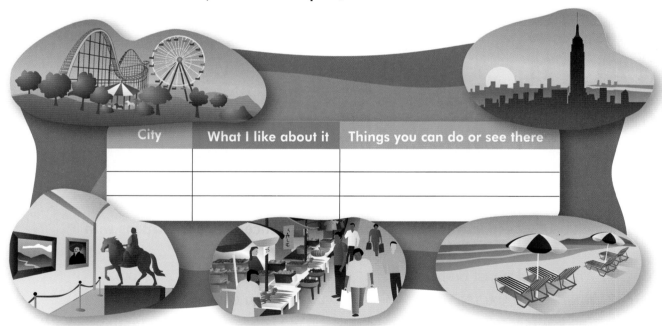

City	What I like about it	Things you can do or see there

B. Groups. Discuss your answers from A with your group members. Ask and answer questions.

A: *One of the places I like in Korea is Pusan.*

B: *What do you like about it?*

A: *I like it because it's near the sea and it has some good beaches.*

B: *What can you do there?*

A: *Well, the shopping is good, and you can also see some beautiful old temples. Also…*

LESSON 2: On vacation

1 VACATION ACTIVITIES

 Track 34 **A.** Look at some of the things you can do when you visit a new city. Circle the things you like to do. Then listen and repeat.

1. visit an amusement park

2. go window shopping

3. go to a night market

4. hear live music

5. go to a nightclub

6. try local food

7. take a city tour

8. look for interesting souvenirs

9. go to the zoo

B. Pairs. Tell your partner about things from A that you like to do.

A: *I like to hear live music.*
B: *Oh you do? I do too. I also like trying local food.*

C. Pairs. Talk with a partner. What else do you like to do when you visit a new city?

A: *Do you usually like to take a city tour?*
B: *Yes I do. I like to take a bus tour with a guide, and then I check out the stores.*
A: *I like to look for interesting souvenirs. I also usually try to see a show.*

2 CONVERSATION STRATEGY: GIVING MORE INFORMATION

 A. Pairs. Listen to the conversations. Then practice with a partner.

1. **A:** When you visit a place, do you like to shop for souvenirs?
   B: Yes, I do. I like to try to buy small gifts for my family.

2. **A:** In a new city, do you like to try the local food?
   B: Yes, I do. I usually ask someone for the name of a good restaurant.

3. **A:** Do you usually check out the stores?
   B: No, I don't. I prefer to go sightseeing.

4. **A:** Do you ever rent a bicycle to look around?
   B: Yes, I do. I think you see a lot more that way.

5. **A:** Do you like to see cultural shows?
   B: Yes, I do. I find them really interesting.

6. **A:** Do you like to travel with someone else?
   B: No, I don't actually. I prefer to be by myself.

B. Notice how we often answer a question by saying *yes* or *no* and giving extra information. Here are some examples of extra information:

I enjoy listening to local music and watching local dances.
I always feel you can meet more people when you're alone.
I like to walk around and see the city instead.
I think it's the best way to get around.
I like to buy local handicrafts.
I like to go to food stalls and try different things there.

Pairs. Now practice the conversations in A again, answering the questions in diffeent ways.

C. Pairs. Use words from A and B to give more information in these conversations. (Different answers are possible.) Then practice with a partner.

1. **A:** Do you often go to museums?
   B: _____ , I don't. _____.

2. **A:** Do you like looking for interesting souvenirs.
   B: Yes, I _____. I usually _____.

3. **A:** When you visit someplace new, do you ever go to the zoo?
   B: No, I _____. I prefer _____.

D. Practice the conversations in A again. This time give your own extra information.

3 LISTEN AND UNDERSTAND

CD 2 Track 36 **A.** Listen to people answering questions about things they do or don't do when they visit a city. Check (✓) if they give extra information when they answer.

	Extra information	No extra information	Topic
1.			
2.			
3.			
4.			

B. Listen again. When the speaker gives extra information, what is the information about? Write *a*, *b*, or *c* under *Topic* in the chart in A.

1. **a.** places **b.** animals **c.** birds
2. **a.** the location **b.** the food **c.** people
3. **a.** the cost **b.** the brand **c.** the style
4. **a.** locations **b.** prices **c.** reasons

4 JOIN IN

A. Pairs. Look at these tours for places in Harlem, an area of New York City famous for its African-American history, food, and music. Discuss which tour you prefer and why.

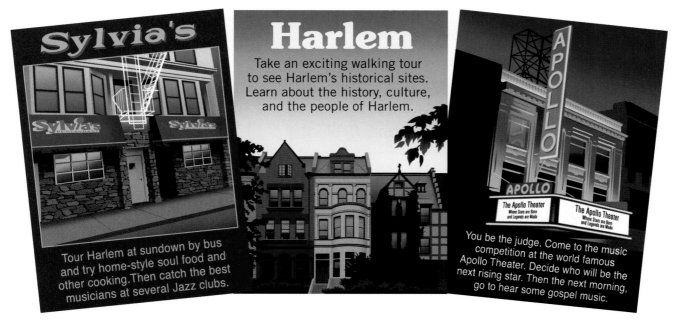

A: Which tour do you prefer?

B: I like the Harlem tour. I like to learn about history and culture. Which do you prefer?

B. Groups. What is the most interesting tour visitors to your city can take? Discuss your opinions with your group.

LESSON 1: Childhood days

1 TELL ME ABOUT YOURSELF

A. Where do you think these people study? Number the pictures below.

1. junior high school
2. university
3. senior high school
4. adult education center
5. grade school

CD 2 Track 37 **B. Listen to the conversation. Then practice with a partner.**

A: Where were you born, Kay?

B: 1 I was born in Osaka, in Japan.

A: Really? And did you learn English at school?

B: 2 Yes, I did. My teacher was from California.

A: That's interesting. And when did you graduate from college?

B: 3 I graduated last year.

C. Pairs. Practice the conversation again. Use this information.

Practice 1

1 I was born in Shanghai, but I grew up in Beijing.

2 Yes, I did, but I also studied for a year in the U.S.

3 I graduated two years ago.

Practice 2

1 I was born in Taiwan.

2 Yes, I did. I started studying English in grade school.

3 I graduated this year.

Track 38 **A.** **Listen and practice.**

Where *were you* born?	*I was* born in China.
Were you born in Beijing?	No, *I was* born in Shanghai.
Where *did you grow* up?	*I grew up* in Hong Kong.
Did you go to high school here?	Yes, *I did*.
	No, *I didn't*. *I went* to high school in Canada.

 Track 39 **B.** **Pairs. Complete the conversations with items from A. Listen and check your answers. Then practice with a partner.**

1. **A:** Where _____ you born?
   B: I _____ born in Bangkok.

2. **A:** Where _____ you grow up?
   B: I _____ up in Toronto.

3. **A:** _____ you study English at school?
   B: Yes, I did. I _____ it in elementary school and high school.

4. **A:** _____ you good at English at school?
   B: Yes, I was.

5. **A:** _____ you enjoy high school?
   B: Yes, I did. I _____ it a lot.

6. **A:** Did you play many sports in high school?
   B: No, I _____.

7. **A:** When _____ you graduate from high school?
   B: I _____ in 2004.

C. **Pairs. Take turns asking and answering the questions above, using true information.**

3 LISTEN AND UNDERSTAND

CD 2 Track 40 **A. Listen to Paul talking about his childhood and check (✓) if the statements below are True or False.**

	True	False
1. He was born in Los Angeles.	☐	☐
2. He grew up in San Francisco.	☐	☐
3. His family moved when he was three.	☐	☐
4. His mother died when he was still young.	☐	☐
5. He enjoyed going to school.	☐	☐
6. Basketball was his favorite sport at school.	☐	☐
7. He used to watch his mother acting in films.	☐	☐

B. Listen again. What are two more things you learn about Paul?

1. _____

2. _____

4 JOIN IN

A. Complete this form with information about yourself.

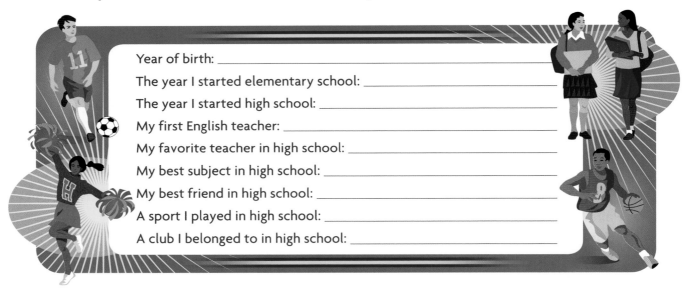

Year of birth: _____

The year I started elementary school: _____

The year I started high school: _____

My first English teacher: _____

My favorite teacher in high school: _____

My best subject in high school: _____

My best friend in high school: _____

A sport I played in high school: _____

A club I belonged to in high school: _____

B. Groups. Interview several classmates and share information from A.

When were you born?

When did you start elementary school?

Who was your first English teacher?

What was your best subject?

Did you play any sports?

Did you belong to any clubs?

1 MILESTONES

  Track 41 **A.** **Look at these important events in Cindy's life. Circle the ones you have experienced. Then listen and repeat.**

1. I got my first bicycle.

2. I got my first pet.

3. I went on my first airplane ride.

4. I learned how to swim.

5. I got my first ATM card.

6. I had my first English lesson.

7. I got my first computer.

8. I got my first cell phone.

9. I got my first ID card.

B. **Pairs. Tell your partner about the activities in A that you have experienced. Ask follow-up questions to find out more.**

A: I got my first bicycle from my parents.
B: Was it for your birthday?

C. **Pairs. What other milestones can you think of? Talk with your partner and make a list.**

A. Pairs. Listen to the conversations. Then practice with a partner.

1. **A:** I got my first bicycle when I was seven.
   B: *Did you? What color was it?* Do you remember?
   A: Sure. I remember it very well. It was silver and black.
   B: Cool.

2. **A:** When did you get your first computer?
   B: When I was 17.
   A: *Really? What kind was it?*
   B: It was an IBM.

B. Notice how we sometimes respond to what people say by asking for more information:

Was it? Did you go by yourself?
Did you? How old were you then?
Oh? What was his name?
Oh, yeah? And where did you fly to?

Pairs. Now practice the conversations in A again, using different expressions to respond and ask for more information.

C. Pairs. Use words from A and B to respond and ask for more information in these conversations. Then practice with a partner and add information of your own.

1. **A:** My first English teacher came from New Zealand.
   B: _____?
   A: I can't remember. But he was really handsome. I remember that.

2. **A:** I learned how to swim in grade school.
   B: _____?
   A: I guess I was about 5.

3. **A:** I took my first flight when I was 10. I was so excited.
   B: _____?
   A: To Pusan. Just an hour away.

4. **A:** I was 15 the first time I went to another city.
   B: _____?
   A: No. I went with my older brother.

D. Pairs. Now tell your partner three things about your past and answer any follow-up questions.

3 LISTEN AND UNDERSTAND

CD 2 Track 43   **A.** Listen to people talking about events they remember. Number the pictures from 1 to 4 in the order you hear about them.

B. Listen again. What do they most remember about each event?

1. **a.** her name and nickname   **b.** what she was good at doing
2. **a.** the country she came from   **b.** the date she left
3. **a.** her car   **b.** the date she graduated
4. **a.** her gift   **b.** her style

4 JOIN IN

A. Class activity. Talk to classmates and find a different person who did each of the following things. Ask them for more information.

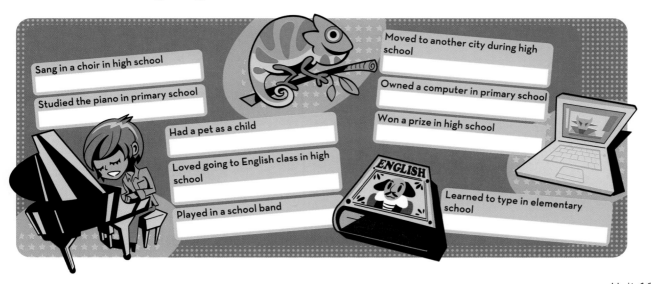

Sang in a choir in high school

Studied the piano in primary school

Had a pet as a child

Loved going to English class in high school

Played in a school band

Moved to another city during high school

Owned a computer in primary school

Won a prize in high school

Learned to type in elementary school

UNIT 5: Lesson 1

4 JOIN IN: STUDENT B

A. Pairs. You are helping correct these records. Ask your partner about the missing information and write it below. Answer Student A's questions. Student B begins.

1.

Name: _____
Occupation: computer technician
Employer: Dot-Com Downtown
Address: _____

2.

Name: Ricardo Jackson
Occupation: _____
School: _____
Major: business administration
Address: 38 East Road, Long Beach

Hi. What's your name?

What do you do?

My name's _____

I _____

B. Pairs. Now practice conversations like the ones in A, using true information about yourself.

UNIT 6: Lesson 1

4 JOIN IN: STUDENT B

A. Pairs. Take turns asking about these locations and mark them on your map. Then check your answers with Student A.

Student B ask about:

1. a bank   **2.** clothing store   **3.** a travel agency   **4.** a taxi stand

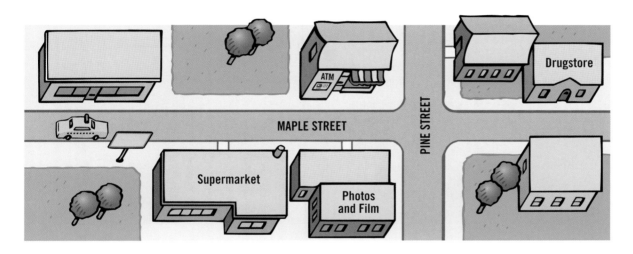

A: Excuse me, I'm looking for _____ .
B: There _____ on the corner of Pine Street and Maple Street.
A: Thanks very much.
B: You're welcome.

4 JOIN IN: STUDENT B

A. **Pairs. Compare your pictures. How many differences are there between the two apartments? Take turns asking your partner about his or her picture. Then check your answers with Student A.**

Does your apartment have three bedrooms?
Is there a dining room and a living room?
Does it have a balcony?

UNIT 7: Lesson 2

4 JOIN IN: STUDENT B

A. Role play. Take turns.

Role play 1

You are a host. Your houseguest asks your permission to do things in your house. Accept or decline the requests. If you decline, give a reason.

Role play 2

You are a houseguest. Here are some things you would like to do. Add two more things to the list. Ask your host for permission.

a. have friends over

b. turn off the air conditioner

c. watch TV

d. come home late

e. use the microwave

f. _____

g. _____

UNIT 10: Lesson 1

4 JOIN IN: STUDENT B

A. Role play. Take turns.

Role play 1

You are a travel agent. An overseas traveler is asking you questions about prices in your country. Answer his or her questions.

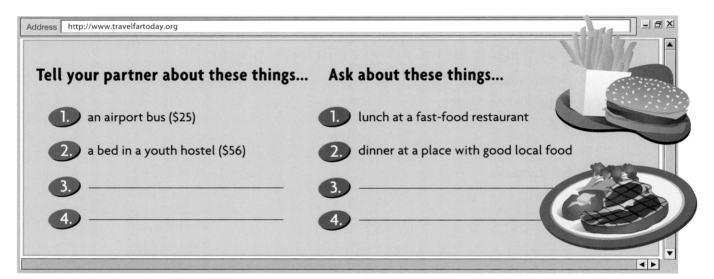

A: *How much is an airport bus?*
B: *I think it costs about...*

Role play 2

You are an overseas traveler talking to a travel agent. You want to know about prices in the country you are going to visit. Add two more items to the list above. Then ask the agent.

B: *How much is lunch at a fast-food restaurant?*
A: *I think...*

Review

UNIT 1

YES/NO QUESTIONS; PRESENT TENSE OF BE

A. Review the language box.

Are you Jack?	Yes, *I am.*
	No, *I'm not.*
Is your last name Wong?	Yes, *it is.*
	No, *it isn't.*
Is he a tennis player?	Yes, *he is.*
Is she a tennis player?	No, *she isn't.*
Are you a student?	Yes, *I am.*
	No, *I'm not.*
Are you from Canada?	Yes, *we are.*
Are you students?	No, *we aren't.*
Are they teachers?	Yes, *they are.*
	No, *they aren't.*

B. Complete the conversations. Use language from Unit 1.

1. **A:** _____ your name Tim?
   B: No, it _____. It's Jon.

2. **A:** Are _____ Jenny?
   B: No, _____ not. I'm Sandy.

3. **A:** Are _____ students?
   B: No, they _____. They are rock singers.
   A: Wow!

4. **A:** Are _____ a tennis player?
   B: No, _____ not. I play basketball.
   A: Cool.

5. **A:** _____ she from Canada?
   B: No, she_____. She's from Australia.
   A: Is that right?

6. **A:** _____ you teachers?
   B: No, we_____.

UNIT 2

BE + ADJECTIVE

A. Review the language box.

What's Toronto like?	*It's* an *interesting* city.
	It's a *big* city.
What's your hometown like?	*It's* not an *interesting* city.
	It's beautiful.
What's your favorite cafe?	King's Cafe. *It's cheap* and *quiet.*
I'm a *good* student.	*We're good* students.
You're a *good* student.	*You're good* students.
She's a *great* teacher.	*They're great* teachers.
He's an *interesting* teacher.	

B. Complete the conversations. Use language from Unit 2.

1. **A:** _____ your hometown like?

   B: It's _____. What about yours?

   A: My hometown is _____.

2. **A:** _____ your school like?

   B: It's _____. And yours?

   A: It's _____.

3. **A:** I like Jo's Cafe. They have good iced coffee. What about you?

   B: I like King's. It's _____.

   A: Oh, that's nice

4. **A:** Is she a good teacher?

   B: Oh, yes. She's very _____.

5. **A:** My favorite music store is The Beat. It's big and very cheap. What's your favorite?

   B: I like Tune Town. It's _____.

6. **A:** What's your favorite class?

   B: English. It's _____.

UNIT 3

ADVERBS OF FREQUENCY

A. Review the language box.

Do you *usually* work late?	Yes, I do.		
	No, I don't.		
Does he *usually* get up early?	Yes, he does.		
she	No, she doesn't.		
What time do you *usually* finish work?	I	*always*	finish work around 6.
		usually	
		often	
		sometimes	
		never	

B. Complete the conversations. Use language from Unit 3.

1. **A:** What time do you get up?
   B: I _____ get up early.

2. **A:** What time do you usually start school?
   B: I _____ start at _____.

3. **A:** What time do you leave school?
   B: I _____ leave at _____.

4. **A:** What time do you _____ get home?
   B: I _____ get home at _____.

5. **A:** Would you like to go to a dance club on Saturday?
   B: Sorry, I can't. I _____ visit my family on Saturday.
   A: OK. How about Friday?
   B: Sure. That sounds fun.

6. **A:** Do you go to dance clubs often?
   B: I _____ go to dance clubs.

7. **A:** I often see a movie on Fridays. Do you want to go to a movie on Friday night?
   B: Thanks. _____.

UNIT 4

COUNT AND NON-COUNT NOUNS

A. Review the language box.

Count	
I like *tomatoes*.	We like *oranges*.
I don't like *carrots*.	You don't like *nuts*.
I don't like them at all.	He doesn't like them at all.
Do you eat *many cookies?*	Yes, I eat *a lot*.
	No, I don't eat *many/any*.
Does he eat many cookies?	Yes, he eats *a lot*.
	No, he doesn't eat *many/any*.
oranges, nuts, bananas, vegetables, mangoes, strawberries	
Non-count	
I like *rice*.	She likes *rice*.
I don't like *broccoli*.	He doesn't like *broccoli*.
I don't like it very much.	They don't like it very much.
Do you drink *much coffee?*	Yes, I drink *a lot*.
	No, I don't drink *much/any*.
Does she drink *much coffee?*	Yes, She drinks a lot.
	No, she doesn't drink *much/any*.
milk, cheese, bread, tea, yogurt, meat, fruit	

B. Complete the conversations. Use language from Unit 4.

1. **A:** Do you drink _____ tea?

   B: Yes, I drink _____.

2. **A:** I love fruit. I eat it a lot. What about you?

   B: Fruit? Yes, I _____ have fruit for dessert.

3. **A:** Are you a vegetarian?

   B: No, I'm not. Actually, I love fish—I eat it _____.

4. **A:** Can I get you a drink?

   B: Yes, please. Do you have _____ soda?

   A: _____? Sure. And would you like some cookies?

   B: No, thanks. I don't _____ cookies.

UNIT 5

WH- QUESTIONS

A. Review the language box.

What do you do?	I'm a student.
	We're gym instructors.
	She works in a hotel.
	They're teachers.
Where do you work?	I work in a hotel.
	I work for City Bank.
Where does he work?	He works in a hotel.
Where do you go to school?	I go to City College.
Where does she go to school?	She studies at State University.
What are you studying?	I'm studying business.
What are they studying?	They're studying music.
Where do you live?	I live downtown.
	We live downtown.
When do you finish your course?	I graduate next year.

B. Complete the conversations. Use language from Unit 5.

1. **A:** _____ are you studying?
   B: I'm studying _____.

2. **A:** _____ do you do?
   B: I _____.

3. **A:** _____ does Terry do?
   B: She's a _____. She loves animals.
   A: That's interesting.

4. **A:** _____ does Bob do?
   B: He's a flight attendant.
   A: Really? It sounds difficult.
   B: He likes it. He gets to travel a lot.
   A: Oh, I'm not sure I'd like that.

UNIT 6

THERE IS / THERE ARE + PREPOSITIONS OF PLACE

A. **Review the language box.**

Where's the subway station?	*There's* one	*down* the street.
		next to the department store.
		across from the hotel.
		on the corner.
	There's an	ATM *in* the mall.
	There's a	music store *on* the corner.
Where are the fast-food places?	*There are* some	*in* the mall.
		near the station.
		on King Street.
	There are some	mailboxes *near* the post office.
		statues *in* the park.

B. **Complete the conversations. Use language from Unit 6.**

1. **A:** Excuse me. _____ can I find a supermarket?

   B: _____ one on Main Street, next to the hotel.

   A: Thanks a lot.

   B: You're welcome.

2. **A:** _____ the post office?

   B: _____ one on Main Street _____ the hotel.

   A: Thank you.

3. **A:** Excuse me. How can I get to the stadium?

   B: _____ a bus stop on the corner of Main and Spring.
   The bus goes to the stadium.

   A: _____ a bus stop on Main and Spring?

   B: Yes, that's right.

4. **A:** Excuse me. _____ King's Park? Is it near here?

   B: It's _____ Maple Street. Go down the street and turn right.
   It's _____ the post office.

   A: OK, thanks.

UNIT 7

QUESTIONS WITH *IS / ARE THERE* AND DOES

A. Review the language box.

Is there	a view?	Yes, there is.
	a yard?	No, there isn't.
Are there	three bedrooms?	Yes, there are.
	two bathrooms?	No, there aren't.
Does it *have*	a balcony?	Yes, it does.
	an elevator?	No, it doesn't.
Does it *have*	a dining room?	Yes, it does.
Is there	a dining room?	Yes, there is.

It doesn't have an elevator.	It has a dining room.
There isn't a swimming pool.	There is a balcony.
There aren't any parking spaces.	There are two floors.

B. Complete the conversations. Use language from Unit 7.

1. **A:** What's your apartment like?

   B: It's not big, but I like it.

   A: Oh, good. How many bedrooms _____ it have?

   B: _____ two bedrooms.

   A: And _____ it have a dining room?

   B: No, it doesn't. But there's a large kitchen.

2. **A:** What's your new apartment like?

   B: It's great! I really like it.

   A: That's great! _____ it have a view?

   B: Yes, _____ a view of the city.

   A: Oh, nice. And _____ a pool?

   B: Yes, _____ . It's fantastic.

   A: Oh, yeah? Is it all right if I come swimming sometime?

   B: Sure.

3. **A:** _____ your apartment have a balcony?

   B: No, _____, but _____ a yard.

   A: Oh, that's nice.

UNIT 8

ADVERB PHRASES

A. **Review the language box.**

How often do you use your camera?	I use it *all the time*.
Do you use your camera very often?	I use it *pretty often/a lot*.
Do you use it a lot?	I use it *from time to time*.
	I don't use it *very often*.
	I *hardly ever* use it.
	I never use it.
How often does he talk on his cell phone?	Oh, he talks *all the time*.
How often does she study?	She studies *a lot*.
Do you send text messages very often?	We send text messages *from time to time*.
Do they take a bus very often?	They *hardly ever* take a bus.

B. **Complete the conversations. Use language from Unit 8.**

1. **A:** Hey, Sam. Do you use your camera very often?
   B: Not really. I _____ use it.

2. **A:** Does Tina have an MP3 player?
   B: Oh, yeah. And she uses it _____. She's always listening to music.

3. **A:** Hi, Morgan. What's that?
   B: It's my new cell phone.
   A: Yeah? It looks great. Do you use it _____?
   B: Oh, yes. I use it _____! I can take photos, listen to music, and make phone calls on it.
   A: Wow, that's really cool.

4. **A:** How often do you go to a bookstore?
   B: I like reading, but I _____ go to a bookstore. I usually get books from the library.

5. **A:** How often do they play sports?
   B: They love sports so they play _____ — almost every day.

UNIT 9

VERB + GERUND

A. Review the language box.

I	love	swimming.
	enjoy	camping.
You	like	white-water rafting.
	don't mind	canoeing.
We	don't like	skiing.
	can't stand	sailing.
They	hate	snow-boarding.
She	loves	swimming.
	enjoys	camping.
	likes	white-water rafting.
He	doesn't mind	canoeing.
	doesn't like	skiing.
	can't stand	sailing.
	hates	snow-boarding.

B. Complete the conversations. Use language from Unit 9.

1. **A:** Do you ever go jogging?
   B: No, I don't really _____ jogging. What about you?
   A: Yes, I _____ jogging.

2. **A:** Do you _____ mountain biking?
   B: Mountain biking? I don't know; I've never tried it.

3. **A:** Emma _____ camping. She goes on a camping trip every summer.
   B: Camping? Oh, I don't _____ it very much.

4. **A:** Tom _____ cooking. He cooks every night. But I _____ cooking.
   B: I don't mind cooking, but I _____washing the dishes!

5. **A:** I _____ horseback riding, but I don't know where to go.
   B: Oh, you can go _____ _____ in the park. It's nice there.

UNIT 10

QUESTIONS WITH *HOW MUCH*

A. Review the language box.

How much is the digital camera?	It's $69.
How much does a CD player cost?	It costs about $170.
How much are these MP3 players?	They're $85.
How much do those DVD players cost?	They're $60.

B. Complete the conversations. Use language from Unit 10.

1. **A:** _____ _____ does the TV cost?

   B: It costs $1,299.

   A: Really? That's quite expensive.

2. **A:** Wow. Look at these sandals. I love the color.

   B: Yes, they're nice. _____ much _____ they cost?

   A: Oh! They're $25. That's not too bad.

   B: You're right. I think you should buy them.

3. **A:** Excuse me. How much _____ the CDs?

   B: _____ all $19.

   A: OK, thanks.

4. **A:** I need some flu medicine. _____ _____ is this?

   B: These tablets are $7.99, sir.

   A: OK, I'll take it.

5. **A:** Excuse me. How _____ are the video games?

   B: Let me see… _____ $19.99 each.

   A: Thanks, I'll take this one, please.

6. **A:** How _____ _____ a movie ticket cost?

   B: Oh, it's not expensive—about $13.

   A: No, that's not bad.

UNIT 11

MODAL VERBS

A. Review the language box.

What *can you* do in Hanoi?	*You can* rent a bicycle.
	You can take a city tour.
Can you take a canal tour?	Yes, *you can*.
	No, *you can't*.
What *should I* do?	*You should go* to the museums.
What *should I* see?	*You should see* the Ho Chi Minh Memorial.
Should I take credit cards?	Yes, *you should*.
	No, *you don't need* to.
What *can they* do in Hanoi?	*They can try* local food at the night market.
Where *can she* buy souvenirs?	*She can buy* local handicrafts downtown.
Should he rent a car?	No, *he shouldn't* (rent a car).

B. Complete the conversations. Use language from Unit 11.

1. **A:** When I visit a new place, I like to rent a bicycle.
   B: Really? Why is that?
   A: I _____ see more of the area that way.

2. **A:** I'm going to Taiwan for vacation. Should I take credit cards?
   B: Yes, you _____.

3. **A:** My mom is going to Singapore next month.
   B: Oh, she _____ visit Sentosa Island. It's beautiful.
   A: OK. What else can she do there?
   B: Oh, she _____ take a night safari at the zoo. It's fantastic!
   A: Wow, that sounds cool. I'll tell her.

UNIT 12

SIMPLE PAST TENSE

A. Review the language box.

Where *were you* born?	*I was* born in China.
Where *was he* born?	*He was* born in Canada.
Where *was she* born?	*She was* born in London.
Were you born in Beijing?	No, *I was* born in Shanghai.
Were they born in Los Angeles?	Yes, *they were.*
	No, *they were born* in San Francisco.
Where *did you grow up*?	*I grew up* in Hong Kong.
	We grew up in Boston.
Did you go to high school here?	Yes, I did.
	No, *I didn't.* I went to high school in Canada.
When *did you move* to Los Angeles?	My *family* moved here when I was three.
When *did she get* her first bicycle?	*She got* her first bicycle when *she was* seven.

B. Complete the conversations. Use language from Unit 12.

1. **A:** I _____ my first bicycle when I _____ five.

   B: Yeah? What color _____ it?

   A: It _____ blue. I loved it.

2. **A:** Do you have a pet?

   B: No, but I _____ a dog when I was young.

   A: Oh, yeah? What _____ its name?

   B: His name _____ Roscoe. He was very friendly.

3. **A:** Sanjay is a good tennis player.

   B: Yes, he _____ on the school team when he was in high school.

   A: Is that right?

4. **A:** Where _____ you born, Cindy?

   B: I _____ born in New Zealand.

   A: Oh, yeah? When _____ you move here?

   B: I _____ here when I was 17.

Vocabulary

UNIT 1

are
baseball
be
classical
country (music)
eating out
first name
is
jazz
last name
music
phone number
reading
rock (music)
shopping
sports
swimming
television
tennis
video games

UNIT 2

beautiful
bookstore
cafe
clean
clothing store
crowded
department store
electronics store
exciting
favorite

hometown
ice-cream shop
interesting
Internet cafe
music
music store
play (*v*)
sporting goods store
sports

UNIT 3

always
around
barbecue
coffee
dance club
fashion show
finish
get together
get up
IT fair
late
leave
movie
never
often
rock concert
science museum
soccer game
sometimes
text (*v*)
theme park
yoga

UNIT 4

appetizer
banana
beverage
bread
broccoli
carrot
cheese
cookie
dessert
fish
fruit
ice cream
mango
meat
milk
nut
orange (*n*)
pie
rice
salad
soda
soup
steak
strawberry
tea
tomato
vegetable
yogurt

UNIT 5

business
computer programmer
DJ
fashion design
flight attendant
hotel clerk
languages
music teacher
rock musician
security guard
singer
software design
student
study (*v*)
tour guide
travel agent
vet
what
when
where

UNIT 6

across from
apartment building
ATM
bridge (*n*)
bus stop
camera shop
down (*prep*)
drugstore
food stall
fountain
in
mailbox
movie theater
museum

near
next to
on (*prep*)
park (*n*)
souvenir shop
stadium
statue
subway station
supermarket
taxi stand
temple
there are
there's
train station
where

UNIT 7

balcony
bathroom
bedroom
come home
computer
dining room
elevator
first floor
have (someone) over (*v*)
help
kitchen
living room
lobby
play music
second floor
study (*n*)
swimming pool

use
view (*n*)
wash dishes
washing machine
watch (*v*)
yard

UNIT 8

a lot (*adv*)
all the time
backpack
belt
bike
camcorder
cell phone
digital camera
electronic dictionary
flexible tripod
from time to time
hardly ever
hybrid vehicle
motorized scuba bike
MP3 player
never
not very often
pedometer
pretty often
robot dog
scanner
skateboard
sunglasses
wave keyboard

UNIT 9

(don't) mind (*v*)
bicycling
bodysurfing
can't stand
canoeing
enjoy
hate
hiking
horseback riding
ice hockey
ice-skating
jogging
love
mountain biking
rock climbing
sailing
skate-boarding
skiing
snorkeling
snowboarding
swimming
tennis
walking
water-skiing
white-water rafting

UNIT 10

airport bus
bakery
batteries
bracelet
breakfast cereal

cake
CD player
clock
clothing store
DVD player
flu medicine
headphones
jewelry store
laptop
magazines
pet food
printer
ring
speakers
sports shoes
tennis balls
T-shirt
watch (*n*)
youth hostel

UNIT 11

amusement park
buy
handicrafts
hear
live music
local food
look for
market
nightclub
rent (*v*)
see (*v*)
take (a tour)
try

visit (*v*)

window shopping

zoo

can (*v*)

should

need (*v*)

UNIT 12

adult education center

airplane

ATM card

born

English lesson

grade school

ID card

junior high school

learn

milestones

pet

senior high school

university

was

were

graduate (*v*)

year

Student CD Track List

This CD contains highlights from each unit
plus new conversations for extra practice.

Unit	Track	Content
	1	Title and copyright
1	2	Page 6, Activity B
	3	Page 6, Activity C, Practice 1
	4	Page 6, Activity C, Practice 2
2	5	Page 12, Activity B
	6	Page 12, Activity C, Practice 1
	7	Page 12, Activity C, Practice 2
3	8	Page 18, Activity B
	9	Page 18, Activity C, Practice 1
	10	Page 18, Activity C, Practice 2
4	11	Page 24, Activity B
	12	Page 24, Activity C, Practice 1
	13	Page 24, Activity C, Practice 2
5	14	Page 30, Activity B
	15	Page 30, Activity C, Practice 1
	16	Page 30, Activity C, Practice 2
6	17	Page 36, Activity B
	18	Page 36, Activity C, Practice 1
	19	Page 36, Activity C, Practice 2

Unit	Track	Content
7	20	Page 42, Activity B
	21	Page 42, Activity C, Practice 1
	22	Page 42, Activity C, Practice 2
8	23	Page 48, Activity B
	24	Page 48, Activity C, Practice 1
	25	Page 48, Activity C, Practice 2
9	26	Page 54, Activity B
	27	Page 54, Activity C, Practice 1
	28	Page 54, Activity C, Practice 2
10	29	Page 60, Activity B
	30	Page 60, Activity C, Practice 1
	31	Page 60, Activity C, Practice 2
11	32	Page 66, Activity B
	33	Page 66, Activity C, Practice 1
	34	Page 66, Activity C, Practice 2
12	35	Page 72, Activity B
	36	Page 72, Activity C, Practice 1
	37	Page 72, Activity C, Practice 2

A separate Class Audio CD containing the complete
audio program is available for teachers.